STORIES OF
YOUNG PIONEERS

In Their Own Words

Violet T. Kimball

Mountain Press Publishing Company
Missoula, Montana

Fifth Printing, September 2009

Map by William L. Nelson
Photo of lantern by Scott Breum

Library of Congress Cataloging-in-Publication Data

Kimball, Violet T.
  Stories of young pioneers in their own words / Violet T. Kimball.
    p. cm.
Includes bibliographical references and index.
  ISBN 978-0-87842-423-8 (alk. paper)
1. Overland journeys to the Pacific—Juvenile literature. 2. Overland Trails
—History—Juvenile literature. 3. Frontier and pioneer life—West (U.S.)—Ju-
venile literature. 4. West (U.S.)—Description and travel—Juvenile literature.
5. West (U.S.)—Biography—Juvenile literature. 6. Pioneer children—West
(U.S.)—Social life and customs—Juvenile literature. 7. Pioneer children—West
(U.S.)—Biography—Juvenile literature. [1. Overland journeys to the Pacific.
2. Frontier and pioneer life—West (U.S.) 3. West (U.S.)—History. 4. Pioneers.]
I. Title.
F593 .K54 2000
978′ .02–dc21

00-010410

PRINTED IN THE U.S.A.

MP Mountain Press
PUBLISHING COMPANY
P.O. Box 2399 • Missoula, MT 59806 • 406-728-1900
800-234-5308 • info@mtnpress.com
www.mountain-press.com

Dedicated to my grandchildren:

Jessica C. Hunt, Alicia H. Hupp, Grant Montgomery, Kyle S. Hunt, Justin C. Hupp, Clayton Hunt, David Montgomery, Dallin Hupp, and Laura Montgomery

May you meet life's challenges with the courage and fortitude of the young people featured in this book.

Praise for
STORIES OF
YOUNG PIONEERS

"I think this book offers a unique way to learn about pioneer life. The true stories told by people who actually traveled across the plains made the journey come to life for me. This would have been a great book to have when we were studying about the pioneers in school."

—Calvin, age 12
OVERLAND PARK, KANSAS

"I thought this book was very exciting and informative! I really liked this book because of the real person accounts!"

—Courtney, age 13,
MARYSVILLE, WASHINGTON

"I never liked historical books before I read this book. I thought it was very interesting and fun to read because I was learning at the same time."

—Megan, age 12
ALPHARETTA, GEORGIA

"I really enjoyed the third chapter called Fun and Recreation. I thought that it was fun to read about what types of games children played back then, and to try to think of a game children still play today that may be similar.... I think if you enjoy reading, you would really enjoy this book!"

—Barbara, age 12,
ST. LOUIS, MISSOURI

"Stories of Young Pioneers is a great book that puts you in the place of young people heading west on the Oregon Trail."

—Caroline, age 10,
RIVERSIDE, CONNECTICUT

"I like how [the] book shows the children's points of view and how there are different people with their own stories in the book, each one different from the next."

—Colin, age 14,
MISSOULA, MONTANA

"I liked the book very much. What an interesting way to learn about history and how people lived! I think many children will like this book. It is informative, funny, and exciting."

—Jessica, age 12
PAHRUMP, NEVADA

"This book was like no other. It is filled with the thoughts of how the pioneer children really felt. It is way better than any history text book."

—Andrew, age 14
CAMP HILL, PENNSYLVANIA

CONTENTS

ACKNOWLEDGMENTS

I wish to take this occasion to acknowledge the help of many who offered great assistance.

Much appreciation goes to Hope Myer and her capable interlibrary loan staff at Southern Illinois University at Edwardsville, who supplied me with many articles and books. I wish to thank the staff at LDS Archives in Salt Lake City; the assistants at the Merrill Mattes Collection at the National Frontier Trail Center in Independence, Missouri; Peter J. Blodgett, curator of western historical manuscripts at the Huntington Library, San Marino, California; and the staff at the Newberry Library in Chicago and the Bancroft Library at Berkeley, California.

Dozens of friends and relatives gave encouragement and rendered expert editorial assistance to help bring this book to completion. Joan Hart, Judy Loyd, and Lois McCullen were instrumental in pushing it forward. My daughter April Kimball Hunt volunteered to read and edit several chapters. My other children, Kay Kimball, Hope Montgomery, and Chase Kimball, cheered me on. Many thanks to my editor at Mountain Press, Gwen McKenna, who brought order out of chaos.

A special thanks and great appreciation go to three trail experts— Lyndia McDowell Carter, David Bigler, and Jeanne Watson. Jeanne read my entire manuscript, made helpful suggestions and corrections, and caught many "greenhorn" errors. What an incredible favor she performed by agreeing to read this book. My thanks "runneth over."

My husband, Stanley, who has spent part of the last twenty-five years in the Mormon Church archives and as a guide on the Mormon Trail, put one thousand primary sources at my fingertips and invited me to accompany him on many trail explorations. This is as much his book as mine.

The author is responsible for errors in fact, judgment, and interpretation.

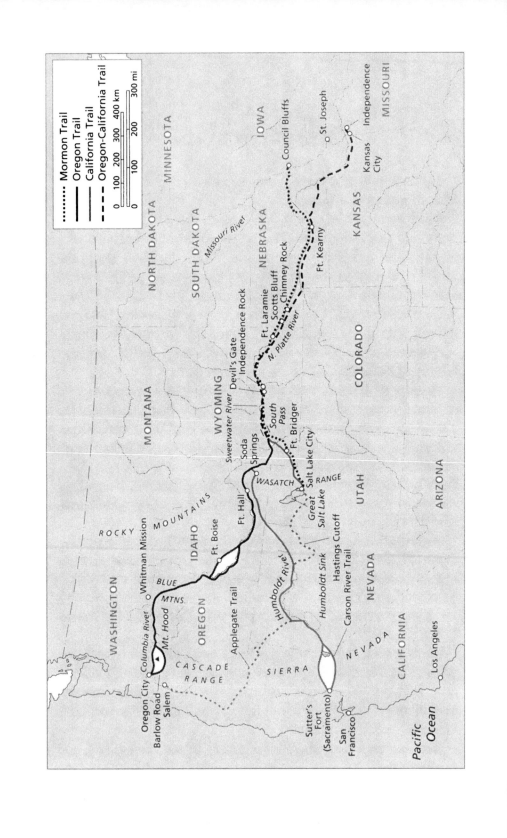

Introduction

Thousands of American families, along with immigrants from Europe and elsewhere, headed west on the Overland Trail in the mid-nineteenth century, toward what they hoped would be a better life. Among these pioneers, about half were young people eighteen and under. This book tells their story.

The trail from Independence, Missouri, to Oregon or California was about two thousand miles long, and from Council Bluffs, Iowa, to Utah was over one thousand. Most emigrant families walked almost the entire way. The walk took them over scorching desert

An Oregon Trail marker at Courthouse Square in Independence, Missouri. —Courtesy Stanley Kimball

sands and craggy, snow-covered mountains, through all kinds of weather. Some children even walked in their bare feet or with only rags tied around their feet, as their parents couldn't afford shoes. The pioneers took baths in icy rivers, killed and ate wild game, and often feared for their lives from wild animal attacks, disease, exposure, and starvation. Many had heard stories of hostile Indians robbing, kidnapping, and murdering white emigrants. In truth, many Native Americans offered the travelers assistance and friendship.

The emigrants, including the young ones, often kept journals of their remarkable journey, and history has been well served by these records. The keen observations of seventeen-year-old Abigail Scott brim with vitality, bringing the romance and poetry of the trail to life. The tragedy of the Donner-Reed party was more vividly rendered by the awkward, poorly spelled correspondence of thirteen-year-old Virginia Reed than by any other account.

Based on over five hundred diaries, journals, letters, reminiscences, autobiographies, and memoirs, this book celebrates the strength and courage these young pioneers showed during the great western migration that occurred between 1842 and 1868. Historians have largely ignored the experiences of young people, but this study reveals how hard they worked, how courageous they often were, and how much they contributed to the success of western settlement. Pioneer children helped make history.

The Lure of the West

By the 1840s, "Oregon fever" was spreading like an epidemic. The only cure was packing the family wagon and turning the team toward the Pacific Ocean. Many children growing up during that time heard their parents discussing this far-off country somewhere out west. Some American missionaries and a few pioneers were out there already, and their letters home raved about the warm weather, the rich soil, the acres of available land, and the spectacular beauty of the northwestern coast. It sounded like paradise.

The successful expedition into what is now the northwestern United States by explorers Lewis and Clark from 1804 to 1806 had created in some Americans a burning desire to populate the area before the British got there. In 1846 Great Britain agreed to cede the region generally known as the Oregon Territory—which included present-day Oregon, Washington, and most of Idaho—to the United States, while they kept the land to the north. The U.S. government encouraged its citizens to move to the territory by offering several hundred acres of free land to anyone who would build a home and settle there. Free land! In spite of the risks, many people jumped at the chance. The ultimate goal was to expand U.S. borders from coast to coast. This idea was known as manifest destiny.

American families began to dream of going west, and a few began to pack. Some western-bound wagons bore signs saying "Oregon or Bust." The very first family to travel overland was Joel and Mary Walker and their five children. In 1840 they packed up a few belongings in their wagon while their horrified Missouri neighbors proclaimed their plan a foolhardy and dangerous undertaking. Paying no attention, the Walkers left with a small company that included Father Pierre-Jean De Smet, a Catholic missionary to Indians in present Montana and Idaho.

The family had little idea what lay between Missouri and Oregon. Their adventure took them across desolate prairies, raging rivers, wide valleys, and towering mountains before they reached their destination. Because the Walkers could not make it across the rugged country beyond Fort Hall, in present Idaho, with their wagons, they had to leave them at the fort. They traveled the rest of the way to Oregon on foot and pack mules. In spite of the difficulties of the journey west, many more families followed the Walkers' lead, and the pioneer movement continued going strong for over twenty-five more years.

Oregon represented only one lure westward. The discovery of gold caused a stampede to California in 1849, and more discoveries followed. Disease in the Midwest also sent thousands to the coast, hoping the warm climate would be therapeutic. Beginning in 1846, the Mormons—members of the Church of Jesus Christ of Latter-day Saints, sometimes simply called Saints—joined the migration, fleeing religious persecution in Nauvoo, Illinois. The church's leader, Brigham Young, led the first exodus to Zion, the promised land, in present-day Utah. Many other Mormons followed.

In 1856 a new stream of Mormons—converts from Europe—increased traffic on the trail west. The Utah Saints started a special fund to help bring these European followers to Zion. Church officials told the Europeans that when they arrived in America, those too poor to purchase horses or oxen should load their possessions into handcarts and pull them the entire 1,300 miles of the Mormon Trail. The church called this effort the "divine plan." The news of the plan spread like a giant wave across the British Isles and into Scandinavia, Germany, Switzerland, and Italy. An official letter from Mormon leaders in Europe stated, "The saints are rejoicing in the anticipation of pulling or pushing a handcart to their home."

Trying Times

In those days, society's attitude toward children was very different from what it is today. Most children were expected to be "seen but not heard" by adults, and discipline was often physical. At the same time, however, youngsters shouldered major responsibilities in the household. On the trail, life was even harder. In addition to the physical exertion of the trip and the countless tasks they had to attend to, many pioneer children witnessed the entire cycle of life and death during the trek west, almost on a daily basis. While a baby was being born in one camp, a marriage was taking place in another, and not far away someone dug a grave for the victim of an all-too-common disease or accident. In addition, many historians contend that because the adults were so preoccupied with the burdens of the difficult journey, children had casual supervision or no supervision at all. Pioneer kids had to fend for themselves.

Accordingly, we learn very little about the young pioneers by reading adult accounts. When adults on the trail stole a few moments to write in their journals at night, there was little time to comment on everyday matters or family life. This lack of informa-

A daguerreotype of two pioneer children, the Chase sisters, circa 1853.
—Courtesy LDS Historical Department Archives

tion about the children has hindered, but not defeated, my quest for their stories. Fortunately, a few of the youngsters kept their own diaries and journals, and some wrote about their experiences later, after they grew up. Others wrote letters or kept notes. I used these and other sources in researching this book. A few of the young people's diaries, including those of Sallie Hester, Abigail Scott, Eliza Ann McAuley, John Steele, Zeb Jacobs, and Welborn Beeson, are particularly descriptive and informative.

In reading their words, I have been impressed, amazed, and moved by these young people, and they seem bigger than life. While some of the adults on the trail acted cowardly and selfish at times, most of the young people remained cheerful and optimistic, viewing the journey as the experience of a lifetime. This book applauds the bravery of not only those we know of, but also of the nameless children who withstood the hunger, pain, and hardships of the trail, often without complaint.

During the course of my study, I walked or drove along all the trails and was able to view much of the landscape seen by the pioneers. I visited all the "jumping-off" places in Missouri, Iowa, and Nebraska. I climbed Independence Rock in Wyoming and photographed some of the signatures there, picked up a real buffalo chip, and walked along the gentle sloping ridge at South Pass, on the Continental Divide. By doing these things I have tried to capture the spirit of place as these hundreds of young people saw and felt it.

Unless otherwise noted, all persons quoted in this book were nineteen or younger when they made the trip west. I made use of adults' diaries when their comments shed light on the discussion at hand. (Although I have eliminated chapter notes, those wishing to do further research will find a complete list of sources cited in the bibliography.) In letting these youngsters speak for themselves, I have maintained their own often unique style of spelling in most cases, although at times I did some minor editing to make the writing more readable. In some cases I changed quotes from third person to first person. Modern readers may find the language of those days oddly formal or otherwise peculiar, yet the genuine feelings come through.

As Abigail Scott, age seventeen, began her trip west in 1852, she wrote:

> *April 2. I am seated by a blazing fire with Heaven's canopy over my head trying to compose my mind and trying [to] . . . form my thoughts into writing by the flickering and uncertain blaze of the large wood fire. . . . [We] are quite anxious to go ahead.*

ONE
Getting Ready

We are all pleased with the Idea of going to oregon. I want to go to see the curiositys and git gold for sewing & to see the buffalo and to hear the wolves howl.

—Letter of Harriet Augusta Stewart, age fifteen, 1854

On May 21, 1843, a large company gathered in the early dawn near Independence, Missouri. Teamsters, trying to get stubborn mules to move forward, cracked their leather whips and swore loudly as the animals kicked and brayed. "Giddup! Giddup!" echoed through the milling crowd while dogs barked, cows wandered, children yelled, and chaos reigned. Finally, the line began to take form, then the wagon master shouted out, more cheerfully, "Wagons Ho!" The call was repeated down the line to the last wagon. They were bound for Oregon.

Men in hats, women in sunbonnets, girls in gingham dresses, and boys in twill shirts, sometimes toting a rifle, inched forward beside the brightly painted wagons. Smaller children sat inside the wagons, watching in wide-eyed wonder. A few men and boys, accompanied by dogs, herded cattle in the rear. As the travelers moved onto the crudely built ferries waiting to cross the Missouri River, the orderly line again began to disintegrate into "oath-filled chaos," as one observer put it.

A replica of a covered freight wagon. —Author photo

Sixteen-year-old Edward Lenox observed a similiar scene as he waited to cross the Missouri with his oxen and wagon at Westport (now Kansas City) that spring. He was one of over one hundred young pioneers following their parents to what they hoped would be a better life. At sixteen, Edward would be allowed a vote in his company's decisions.

A few months earlier, Edward and his father had listened to Peter Burnett, a well-known Missouri lawyer and orator who later became the first governor of California, extol the virtues of Oregon. Standing on a soap box in front of his office, Burnett held his audience captive. Edward later recalled the speech in his memoirs:

> *"Gentlemen, out in Oregon the pigs are running about round and fat, and already cooked. Now gentlemen, walk right into my store and put down your names." My father was the first to sign his name. . . . The farm was soon sold [and] about the most important thing that father did was to buy a yoke of leader oxen that were celebrated leaders in crossing water.*

Edward was in charge of those oxen, and he would soon prove his mettle on the challenging trail ahead. He must have felt both excitement and fear as he moved his wagon and oxen off the ferry and entered present Kansas, which was then Indian territory. Although a few small groups of pioneers had gone before them, Edward's family was part of the first large company to migrate west—a party of several hundred later joined by Christian missionary Marcus Whitman.

The following year, the Sager family, including nine-year-old Catherine, her two older brothers, and her three younger sisters, joined the Oregon Trail migration. Later in her life, Catherine remembered how it all began:

> In 1843 Doctor Whitman had taken a train of emigrant wagons across the Rocky Mountains. This was the theme of much conversation among the neighbors. . . . Father had already become restless, and talked of going to Texas. But mother, hearing much about the healthfulness of Oregon, preferred to go there. . . . It is well that we can not look into the future and see what is before us. Could my parents have done so, how they would have shrunk back from that undertaking.

The Bonney family of Smithfield, Illinois, had various reasons for going west in 1845. One was to flee the "fever and auge" (malaria) that was then raging in the Midwest. Another was to fish for the wonderful salmon they'd heard tell of. "My father loved to fish," recalled Benjamin Bonney, just seven the year they left. The Bonneys started out for Oregon but ended up in California. According to Benjamin, over three thousand people headed west that spring. He remembered the scene when his father announced the family's intentions to the neighbors:

> I can well remember what a hullabaloo the neighbors set up when Father said we were going to Oregon. They told him his family would be killed by Indians, or if we escaped the Indians we would

starve to death, be drowned, or lost in the desert. Father was not a man to pull back after he had put his hand to the plow; so he went ahead and made ready for the trip.

Money troubles motivated some people to go west. Eleven-year-old Lucy Henderson was away at school—Clay Academy—when her father decided to move the family in 1846. The Oregon-boosting attorney Peter Burnett, who had inspired Edward Lenox's father to migrate, also had a hand in Mr. Henderson's decision. Lucy recalled:

When father lost his farm he decided to go where he could have all the land he wanted. . . . He visited a young lawyer, Peter H. Burnett, who advised him to go to Oregon. . . . I knew nothing of this until Father decided to go. Then he came for me and took me out of school, to my deep regret. . . . About 500 wagons started for Oregon that spring.

The Mormon Exodus

February 1846 marked the beginning of the great migration of the Mormons, or Saints. The first Mormons marched west from their headquarters in Nauvoo, Illinois, after suffering religious persecution that had culminated in the murder of their leader, Joseph Smith. Their new leader, Brigham Young, led them first to Council Bluffs, Iowa, then across the Missouri River to current Nebraska, where they stayed the winter. In 1847 they started out toward the Rocky Mountains, to a place they would later call their Zion in what is now Utah, where they could practice their faith in peace.

General George Washington would have been proud of one young Mormon who bore his name. As church leaders prepared the first group to depart Nauvoo, Illinois, and cross the Mississippi River into Iowa, George Washington Bean, age fourteen, helped cut down trees to make the wagons:

10

I was detailed to go over into Iowa to cut and prepare wagon timber of white oak and hickory that grew there in abundance. . . . The timber we hauled nine miles to the river and boated it across.

When the party set out in February, George helped the wagons across the ice-clogged Mississippi. A few weeks later, George's own family prepared to leave Nauvoo.

One young Mormon almost missed the exodus of 1846. Eleven-year-old Edwin Pettit, whose parents had died, wanted to follow the Mormons west, but his guardian would not permit him to leave Nauvoo. After one failed attempt to join a party headed for Council Bluffs, the determined Edwin again plotted his escape:

I got up very early in the morning, and went down stairs with my shoes in my hands. My guardian was dozing in his chair as I slipped out. . . . I lay out in the prairie all night alone. Disguised as a girl, and in company with four or five girls, I crossed the Des Moines River on a flat boat. . . . . I was wearing a wig and side-combs in my hair, and also wearing a sunbonnet in order to make my disguise complete. On landing on the opposite side of the river, an old friend met me on horseback, and took me on behind him. As is well known, girls are supposed to ride sidewise, I also took that precaution.

Edwin made it to Council Bluffs and arrived in the Salt Lake Valley the next year, minus his curls and bonnet.

After the first Mormon group left in February, many more followed. The ones who remained in Nauvoo continued to be severely persecuted. In September 1846, hundreds of men attacked the Mormons who had not yet left the area. Twelve-year-old Sarah Norris's father and her brother Nathaniel, age seventeen, volunteered to defend the town. Their father was killed. Nathaniel stood guard day and night. Their father's body was returned to them, and Sarah sat in vigil with it all night:

Mother [seven months pregnant at the time] had been in poor health all summer and was now prostrated with grief. My little brother Benjamin, five years old, had cried himself to sleep. This left me all alone down stairs with the dead. A tallow candle for light, the blood dripping, dripping from the body all night.

The mob gave them three days to leave:

Later in the day a flag of truce was carried over and a treaty made that all that did not renounce their religion should cross the river in three days. . . . [Soon] the necessary preparations were being made for the journey west.

The family hurried out of town. Sarah's mother and the new baby died two months later.

Starting in 1856, Mormon converts from Europe began to join the American Saints in large numbers, traveling thousands of miles before they even reached the start of the trail. Many came from England and the Scandinavian countries.

Ruth May came from England in 1866, at age eleven:

After a walk of four or five miles under the stars we boarded the train to Liverpool. . . . We had secured berths in the [ship's] steerage which meant that we must descend through a trap door to our quarters below deck. . . . As I remember, there was absolutely no privacy. . . . At last we landed at Castle Garden [New York City].

It was another year before the May family made it all the way to Salt Lake.

Some children even came to America alone. Among the earliest European Mormons to emigrate in 1852 was Nicolean Marie Bertlesen, age seven. Her parents stayed in Denmark and sent Nicolean with a party of Mormon missionaries to join her siblings who were already in Utah. She was told to "keep clean, wait on yourself, and never cry." When they arrived in the United States, the missionaries left Nicolean with a family in St. Louis, promising to tell her relatives in Utah to send for her.

She waited bravely for word from her relatives, but it never came. In the meantime she worked for wages and saved her money. She decided that if she was going to get to Utah, she would have to do it on her own.

After two years of working and saving I had enough money to buy my transportation to Council Bluffs. By this time [she was now age nine] I had also learned to read and write the English language.

In Council Bluffs, a man named Cyrus Snell hired her to help his sick wife and their small children on their way to Utah in exchange for meals along the way. "I walked with the two Snell boys nearly the entire distance to Salt Lake City," Nicolean recalled.

Making Preparations

Before emigrants began the "journey that promised no return," they had to sell most of their property and buy provisions and a "fit out" (a wagon and team). Many people built their own wagons. Families also had to prepare food for the trip. It could take months to get ready, and nearly everyone was involved in the preparations, including the children.

Many years after the fact, William M. Colvig remembered his family's preparations for their trip west:

On May 4, 1851 when I was six years old, we held an auction in our home [in] Platte County, Missouri, and sold everything that Mother did not want to take to Oregon. . . . I can still visualize the family wagon. On a rack, fastened to the hickory wagon bows, was father's Kentucky rifle, and beside it was [gun] powder. . . . On the side of the wagon bed, the coffee mill was fashioned.

Packing for the journey was quite a chore. Emigrants were advised to take the following for a family of three:

Three or four yoke of oxen, one wagon, two if possible, mules and cows, rifles, pistols, five barrels of flour, bacon, coffee, tea, brown sugar, molasses, rice, dried fruit, spices such as salt, pepper and saleratus [baking soda], lead and powder for the guns, tools, tent, bedding, cooking utensils, lard, matches, candles, and soap.

It took about six hundred dollars to prepare a family of three for the journey. Multiply that by ten to get an approximate equivalent in today's money. Most emigrants tried to take extra supplies because prices on the Pacific coast were several times higher.

Benjamin Bonney remembered his father packing their wagon:

He built a large box in his home-made wagon and put in a lot of smoked and pickled pork, 100 pounds of maple sugar [and] plenty of corn meal, a big supply of dried buffalo meat, two gallons of unroasted coffee, and some home-twist tobacco.

Other staples pioneers packed in their wagons included beans, dried bread, apples, and anything else that would last for several months. Another item in some wagons was a chamber pot, which was invented a few thousand years before modern toilets. In addition, the pioneers needed to take plenty of warm clothes and bedding. Most of this was homemade. Women and girls made mattresses and pillows stuffed with goose feathers and sewed quilts using fabric cut from old clothing or leftover scraps. Thirteen-year-old Elizabeth Currier made a quilt in 1845 that she brought to Oregon the next year.

Harriet Augusta Stewart, fifteen, reveals a keen sense of humor in this letter to a cousin about preparing for the trip west in 1854:

We shall take with us 6 feather beds to oregon. . . . Wm [her brother] kills two [cranes] at one shoot. He fetches in ducks and quailes most every day. We feel like thumping [him] for it, for we have them to pick [pluck]. . . . Dad and Jim [another brother] got in such a hurry the other day to go to oregon they sacked up there

Elizabeth Currier (Foster).
—Courtesy Schmink Museum;
photo by Mary Bywater Cross

*Quilt made by
Elizabeth Currier at
age thirteen for her
overland journey in
1845.* —Courtesy Schmink
Museum; photo by Mary
Bywater Cross

*beans and peaches and sewed them up. They wanted to sack up
the apples. . . . We have to sack everything we take even our cloathes.*

Worried neighbors often plagued those who were leaving with
dire warnings about the risk of death on the trail. Moreover, everyone knew that bodies often had to be left in shallow graves in the
middle of nowhere. Most emigrants were horrified at the idea of
being put into the ground without a casket or a shroud (burial
robe). Nine-year-old Barnet Simpson's mother took a burial shroud
for everyone in her family:

When we started across the plains all our neighbors told Mother what a dangerous trip it was and how we were sure to be killed by Indians or drowned or die of cholera or be run over by buffalos. Mother, who had heard how they buried people . . . decided she would be forehanded, so the winter before we left she carded and spun and wove a lot of cloth, dyed it and cut it up and made a shroud a piece for everyone in the family. No, we didn't get to use a single one of them.

Some people preparing to emigrate owned slaves where they lived, but slavery was seldom practiced in the western territories. Many sold the slaves before they left; others freed them. Amanda Gardener, age nineteen, was the slave of a white family going to Oregon in 1853. Her mistress, Mrs. Lydia Deckard, planned to free her upon arrival. Amanda later left this account:

A merchant, hearing that my master was to go to Oregon Territory, where slaves could not be held, came to Mr. Deckard and said: "I will give you $1200 for Amanda. You can't own her where you are going, so you might as well get what you can out of her." Mr. Deckard asked me if I wanted to be given my freedom, but I was afraid to accept my liberty.

Mr. Deckard told the man, "She is the same as one of our family, so I guess I won't sell her." Amanda went to Oregon with the Deckards. She remembered the trip:

When I think back nearly 70 years, I can see herds of shaggy-shouldered buffaloes, slender-legged antelopes, Indians, sagebrush, graves by the roadside, dust and high water and the campfire of buffalo chips over which I cooked the meals.

"The Handcart Company" by C. C. A. Christensen. —Courtesy
Museum of Church History and Art. © Intellectual Reserve

The Divine Plan

According to the Mormon Church's "divine plan," European
Saints were to sail to America and proceed by train to Iowa City,
Iowa, the starting point for the long trek to Utah. From there they
would walk, pushing or pulling all their possessions in handcarts.
Hundreds of European families responded to the plan.

When the European emigrants docked in Boston or New York
City after their trans-Atlantic voyage, those who could afford it
took regular passenger trains to Iowa, while others rode in "cattle
cars," crowded freight trains with no seats. Many had a similar introduction to the Iowa camp as Heber McBride, thirteen, in 1856:

*We took the train for Iowa City. When we got there and our bag-
gage unloaded, it was getting late in the day and our camping
ground was 3 miles from the City ... so a greate many of the people
started for the camp on foot. We had not gon very far when it*

began to rain and was so dark I got lost from the rest of the Company but made out to keep the road by the help of the lightning for Iowa can beat the World for thunder and lightning. After ascending a steep hill I could see a fire.

The families came with feather beds, books, clothing, keepsakes, cookware, and other household items. Upon their arrival in Iowa City, many were shocked to discover they could take only a small number of their belongings in the handcarts. Each adult was limited to a total of seventeen pounds' worth of items; children were allowed ten pounds each.

While some people simply left their things behind in piles, others sold their belongings at bargain prices. As one young Mormon, Mr. Theo Dedrickson, wrote:

We were advised to sell all of our baggage except the bare necessities so we would not have to lug so much along, so I sold my very good collection of bedding and a good trunk for $9.00. The bedding alone was worth $100.00.

The emigrants agonized over which items were really necessities and which they could bear to part with. Mr. John Jaques observed:

It was grievous to see the heaps of books and other articles thus left in the sun and rain and dust, representing a respectable amount of money spent . . . in England.

Painful Partings

Setting out for parts unknown and leaving behind one's home, friends, and relatives was naturally an emotional, even traumatic, experience. The knowledge that one would soon have to say goodbye could make preparing for the trip painful. Katherine (Kate) Scott, then age thirteen, later remembered tears and "trembling fingers" in 1851 and 1852 as she and her family got ready to leave Tremont, Illinois, for Oregon:

Through all the winter preceding the April when the final start was made, the fingers of the women and girls were busy providing additional stores of bedding and blankets, of stockings and sunbonnets, of hickory shirts and gingham aprons that the family might be equipped for the trip. . . . Ah! the tears that fell upon these garments, fashioned with trembling fingers by the flaring light of tallow candles, the heartaches that were stitched and knitted and woven into them, through the brief winter afternoons, as relatives . . . dropped in to lend a hand in the awesome undertaking of getting ready for a journey that promised no return.

Elisha Brooks's family was among the few who went to California after 1849 for its healthful climate rather than for gold. Elisha's description of his family's departure showed more anticipation than sadness, perhaps because he wrote it about seventy years later. In the spring of 1852, Elisha's mother received a letter from his father, who was already in California, urging the family to join him.

My mother loaded all her worldly possessions, consisting of a stock of provisions and a camp outfit, into a canvas covered wagon drawn by four yoke of oxen; and with her little family of five boys, aged three, five, nine, twins of eleven, one of whom was myself, and a girl of thirteen years, she bade goodbye to the old cabin home and the surrounding malarial swamps in St. Joseph County, Michigan, and took up her march of two thousand eight hundred miles, as the road winds, in search of the land of good health, more alluring to us than visions of gold.

Fourteen-year-old Sallie Hester's family also sought health, not gold, in California. Sallie's first diary entry captured a bittersweet farewell to family and friends in Bloomington, Indiana:

March 20, 1849. Our family, consisting of father, mother, two brothers and one sister left this morning for that far and much talked of country, California. . . . The last hours were spent in bidding goodbye to old Friends. My mother is heartbroken over this separation of relatives and friends. . . . My father is going in search of health, not gold. The last good bye has been said, the last glimpse of our old home on the hill, and wave of hand at the old Academy and we are off.

Who were more sad and tearful—the ones who left or the ones who stayed behind? Nothing captures the pain of parting like this excerpt from Kate Scott's memoir:

Memory . . . paints a picture of moving wagons, of whips flourished with many a resounding snap, of men walking beside them with a forced show of indifference, though now and then the back of a brawny hand was drawn hurriedly over the eyes; of silently weeping women and sobbing children, and of an aged grandfather standing at his gate as the wagons filed past, one trembling hand shading his eyes, the other grasping a red handkerchief. . . . "Good-by, good-by." The old grandsire's response was choked with emotion . . . and the little caravan moved on out of sight.

—SUMMARY—

Families had many reasons for leaving their homes to go west—land, gold, health—but all left with high hopes. They made ready for the great undertaking with a mixture of sadness, fear, and anticipation. Of course, the children in these families generally had no choice about whether or not to go. Some cheered their parents' decision; others grieved. Regardless of their feelings, the young people participated fully in the preparations, just as they would soon participate fully in the adventure of the great western migration.

~

Profile of
MARGARET MCNEIL (BALLARD)

Margaret McNeil (Ballard), with her twins, Jeanette and Charles.
—Courtesy Janet G. Ralph

Margaret McNeil, another remarkable young teenager who crossed the plains, probably withstood a few more hardships than most pioneers. Certain events, though, that seemed heaven-sent bolstered her faith and optimism. Margaret's autobiography tells a tale of struggle and triumph.

Margaret was born in Tranent, Scotland, on April 14, 1846, to a coal miner and his wife, Thomas and Janet Reid McNeil. Soon afterward, Margaret's parents joined the Mormon Church. Life was hard in Scotland. Children—especially poor children—got very little education. Religious persecution compounded Margaret's lack of opportunity:

Because of being a Mormon, I was not permitted to attend the schools and so I was entirely deprived of schooling while in the old country.

On April 27, 1856, just after Margaret turned ten, the family left Scotland to join the handcart companies that were organizing to pull their humble possessions to Utah and a better life. The adventures began before they even set sail, as Margaret described in her recollections:

My mother was not well and was taken on board ship before the time of sailing, while the sailors were still disinfecting and renovating the ship. Here my brother Charles was born, with only one woman on board to attend to my mother. . . . He was named Charles Collins Thornton McNeil, after the ship [Thornton] and Captain Charles Collins.

Margaret, as the oldest child, bore some of the burden of the new baby's care. She also helped prepare meals—the passengers did their own cooking on the ship—and looked after the smaller children. Among the other passengers was Mormon missionary James G. Willie, leader of the company the McNeils would travel with to Iowa City. When they disembarked, though, chance or fate intervened: "We landed at Castle Garden, New York, and Franklin D. Richards [a high Mormon official] counseled my father not to go in that company."

Margaret's parents were asked instead to help settle Genoa, Nebraska. Had they set out westward immediately as planned, they would have been in the fifth James Willie Handcart Company, which suffered horrible privation, hunger, cold, isease, and death. Three more years passed before Margaret arrived in Utah. For over two years, the family lived in dugouts and crude cabins in Nebraska.

When the McNeils left Genoa in 1859 to continue their journey to Zion, Margaret, then thirteen, did much to lessen the burdens of her family. She herded and milked the cows, cooked, tended to younger siblings, and walked all the way across the plains, cheerful and accepting.

After their arrival in Utah, the hardships continued:

> We camped in a fort for protection. My father . . . went to the canyons and hauled logs to make a house. We had neither lumber nor glass, so for doors and windows we wove willows together and plastered them with clay. . . . I carried water for the family all winter from the Logan River about three blocks away. I had very little clothing on my body and my feet were bare. I left blood in the snow. Sometimes I would wrap them in old rags, but this was worse than ever because the rags froze on my feet. . . .
>
> At one time we were right out of everything to eat and Father had a few logs he could spare and went to a man and asked if he would not give him some bran for them. This is all we had to eat for some little time. . . . Early in the spring I went to work for one dollar a week. I was working to get seed wheat for us to plant. . . . I went out in the fields to glean so we would have enough bread for the winter.

In 1865 Margaret married Henry Ballard, and her life improved. Several of their children died, but Margaret's faith never wavered. In 1875 she exercised that faith in an unusual religious experience:

> My husband was brought home from the canyon very sick suffering with kidney trouble. The brethren administered to him but he was very, very bad and we thought he was surely dying. I was greatly grieved to see him in such agony. He looked at me and said he knew he could die if I would only give him up. But a voice came to

me and said, "Administer to him," but I was very timid about doing this for the brethren had just administered to him. The voice came again. . . . The third time . . . I heeded to its promptings and went and put my hands upon his head. The spirit of the Holy Ghost was with me and I was filled with a divine strength in performing the ordinance. My husband slept quietly for two hours or more. . . . They often speak of this miraculous healing.

Margaret died in 1918, at age seventy-two. Her great-grandson, M. Russell Ballard, is a high Mormon official today, and many other relatives still live in Utah and around the country.

Daily Life on the Trail

I can still see the plains with the shimmering heat waves, the dark masses of buffalo moving over the rolling hills toward the Platte, the campfires of buffalo chips and later of sagebrush. . . . I walked most of the way across the plains, as did many of the other young folks.

—Remembrance of Eliza McKean, age thirteen in 1847

It was the little things about trail life that most pioneers, like Eliza, remembered for the rest of their lives. Barnet Simpson was nine when he crossed the plains in 1846:

All I need to do today, nearly 80 years later, is to shut my eyes and I can see the vast, empty plains with their rolling land waves. I can see the wagons come to a stop, see the children pile out of the wagons while the men folks unyoke the oxen and all the women scatter to [cook supper].

Depending on the route and on travel conditions, the overland trek took from about four to eight months to complete. The experience of making that journey was full of beauty and adventure, hardships and joy, satisfactions and surprises. In this chapter are portraits of daily life on the trail, descriptions of some of the natural wonders along the route, and a few tales of adventure.

Setting Out

The sadness of leaving their homes behind mingled with the fear of what lay ahead as families set out on their great journey. The first objective once the trek began was to get across the major rivers that lay between their former homes and the western frontier. The emigrants crossed the Missouri River on rickety ferries at Independence or St. Joseph, Missouri, or at Council Bluffs, Iowa. Those coming from Illinois or other areas east of the Mississippi River had to cross the Mississippi first, then tackle the Missouri at Council Bluffs. As soon as they crossed the Missouri, the pioneers were no longer in the official United States. Catherine Sager, then age ten, later described her feelings as she crossed the Missouri:

> In the month of April, 1844, we set out on our long and perilous journey across the plains. . . . We children wept for fear of the mighty waters that came rushing down and seemed as though it would swallow them up. . . . It was a sad company that crossed the Missouri River that spring day.

The Missouri River had a bad reputation. Pioneers referred to it as "Old Muddy Face" and to the bottomland along the river as the "Misery Bottoms." Sallie Hester, crossing this river in 1849 at age fourteen, wrote in her diary:

> On the Missouri River, the worst in the world, sticking on sand bars most of the time. . . . Our boat struck another sand bar and was obliged to land passengers ten miles below St. Joe.

Seventeen-year-old Eliza Ann McAuley, getting ready to cross at Council Bluffs in 1852, discovered how dangerous river crossings could be:

Tues, May 11th. Got up early and took the wagons down a little nearer the ferry, so as to take advantage of the first opportunity to cross. A dreadful accident happened here today. A boat manned by green hands was taking a boat of cattle across. The cattle rushed to one end of the boat, causing it to tip and in a moment there was a mass of struggling men and animals in the water. One man was drowned.

Many saw only the harshness of this river, but Helen Stewart, a seventeen-year-old with romance in her soul, saw its beauty in 1853:

There was such romantic looking rock towering away up it brought me in mind of some old ruined castle I have read about. . . . It was so beautiful on the water when the moon was shineing bright, it added more beauty to the romantic sceniry round.

The Mississippi River was also difficult to cross, as it was quite muddy, and there were many episodes of disaster there. Elisha Brooks, eleven at the time, recalled this 1852 scene:

We crossed the Mississippi River on a little ferry boat, just large enough to hold one wagon and team, propelled by two horses, one on each side of the boat, in a treadmill. . . . It was early spring, and there was mud, mud everywhere—slush to drive through, to eat in, to sleep in.

The Mormons who crossed the Mississippi at Nauvoo, Illinois, in February 1846 found worse than mud in their hurried departure. Unlike most emigrants, who generally left in April or May, some Mormons decided to leave before the spring thaw. A few Saints died in that freezing, snowy, bleak exodus. When the river froze a few weeks later, some emigrants crossed over on the ice, as fourteen-year-old George Bean observed:

About the first of March, the heaviest snow of the winter [fell, and] the Mississippi River was closed. Some said the ice was four feet thick. As the ice broke into large chunks, some animals had a

"Crossing the Frozen Mississippi on Ice" by C. C. A. Christensen.
—Courtesy Museum of Art, Brigham Young University

terrible time to get to shore. . . . One foot of snow covered the ground. The cold was intense [and] the roads were impassable for weeks.

The Mormons made temporary settlements at Council Bluffs, Iowa, and across the Missouri in Winter Quarters, in present Nebraska, and continued their journey to the Salt Lake Valley in April 1847.

Once over the rivers, the official trail began. Here emigrants began to notice the beauty of the landscape. Many diaries and letters comment on the stunning scenery along the trail. In 1852 twelve-year-old Elizabeth Keegan saw the view from a lofty perch on her horse:

The first part of [the trail] is beautiful and surpassing anything of that kind I have ever seen. Large rolling prairies stretching as

far as your eye can carry you. The grass so green and flowers of
every description from violets to geraniums of richest hue.

The lovely scenery might compensate for a messy and uncomfortable departure, yet it could not always ease the pain of leaving beloved people and places behind. Mary Jane Mount, then age nine, remembered the landscape of her first day on the trail in 1847, but she also remembered the sadness:

I think I shall never forget that long lonely day, waiting on that vast undulating prairie that stretched as far as the eye could reach, covered with grass and flowers. . . . It must have been a lovely scene that bright spring morning, but I hardly think it was appreciated by the little band who were so bravely leaving home, friends, country, and kindred, to take their toilsome march across the Rocky Mountains.

Wagons West

Emigrants who left from Missouri stayed south of the Platte River, on the Oregon Trail through Nebraska, while those starting from Council Bluffs, Iowa, remained north of the river. The South Platte route was the main trail for those going to Oregon and California. Brigham Young and his followers mostly used the North Platte route, so it became known as the Mormon Trail. The two trails merged near Fort Laramie, in present Wyoming, where the Oregon Trail pioneers discovered the emigrating Mormons and vice versa. The two groups shared the same trail for hundreds of miles, moving as "villages on wheels." Farther west the trails separated again. The main route to Oregon veered north, while the Mormon Trail and the main California Trail continued southwest. There were also many cutoffs and variations on these routes.

A number of pioneers had fine wagons, while others had only primitive handcarts. During the gold rush, a few desperate men rushed across the continent with wheelbarrows, and some just strapped a pack onto their back. Sometimes families shared a vehicle. One humble farm wagon had to be the winner of the most-people-sharing-a-wagon contest—that of thirteen-year-old Ruth May's 1867 party. Ruth faced the situation with a resolute spirit:

> When we arrived at North Platte, it so happened that a certain brother had a wagon and one yoke of cattle, so the bargain was made that Father join his cattle to this outfit and drive all the way for his share in the wagon. The owner had a wife and seven children. Our little family consisted of five. . . . So you see there were fourteen with all their worldly possession in that one wagon.

Those oxen had a heavy burden, but the families probably had brought little but food and other essentials. Ruth and her family slept in a tent at night, "side by side, like sardines in a can, while the other family of nine slept in the wagon amid all the bedding, clothing and cooking utensils." They must have been double-decked.

The Mormons from Europe who went to Utah with handcarts forged a unique westering experiment. The carts were made of oak or hickory with wooden wheels, and they weighed up to sixty pounds. A few had canvas covers. The emigrants pulled the carts with their bodies as horses would a wagon. In large families several members could work as a team. Mary Powell, almost thirteen, helped her father pull the cart while her brother William pushed from the rear. Inside were two younger Powell children, one hundred pounds of flour, and utensils, clothing, and bedding for their family of seven. Their cart probably weighed over six hundred pounds. The Powells were among the 274 Mormons in Captain Edmund Ellsworth's historic first handcart company, which moved out June 9, 1856, from Iowa City. A second company, under D. D. McArthur, left with 220 Saints two days later.

The ethnic backgrounds of the pioneers were as varied as the United Nations. Immigrants and Americans of German, Swedish, Danish, Italian, Scottish, Irish, Jewish, African American, and other heritages joined the westering movement. In addition, people from

Australia, China, and elsewhere in the Eastern Hemisphere came to the West Coast by sea. Since slavery was still legal in many states, slaves sometimes escaped to the West, but more often they traveled with their owners and gained their freedom upon arrival. Free black citizens from the northern states also went west to seek their fortune.

There were a few free black families in the Mormon exodus of 1846. Isaac and Jane Manning James and their children Sylvester, Vilate, Ellen, Marian, and Jesse were among the Mormons fleeing Nauvoo. In June, not far from Council Bluffs, a new baby joined this family. Mrs. James talked about these experiences in her memoirs:

> *In the spring of 1846 I left Nauvoo. . . . At Keg Creek my son Silas was born. In the spring of 1847 we started again on our way to [the Salt Lake] valley, and we arrived here on 22nd of Sept, 1847 without any serious mishaps.*

Silas was probably the first free black baby born in Iowa Territory, and the Jameses were probably the first free black family to cross the plains.

Walking the Walk

While some of the luckier young pioneers were able to ride horseback for part of the journey, and even more rarely some were allowed to ride in a wagon, most pioneers, adults and children alike, walked virtually the whole way. Many shoes wore out long before the trip was over, and some youngsters could not wear shoes at all because their feet were so sore, swollen, and blistered from walking. Some children's feet became encrusted with blood mixed with alkali sand, turning them black. But even the sturdiest feet suffered when walking about fifteen miles a day, sometimes farther.

One of the barefoot youngsters was seven-year-old Benjamin Bonney, who years later could still recall the pain of stepping on prickly pears along the Humboldt River, which runs through present Nevada, in 1845:

On this sagebrush plain we found lots of prickly pear. We children were barefooted, and I can remember yet how we limped across that desert from piercing the soles of our feet with the sharp spines of this cactus.

Joseph Fish, age ten in 1850, offered this depiction of walking the long, hot, dusty trail:

Bare-footed children, here and there, wending their way along the line of march. Women, some with sunbonnets, some with hats, traveling along through the hot dust and over the parched plains. Men with their long whips walked beside the lolling oxen that were dragging their heavy loads towards the setting sun. . . . The sun and alkali dust [was] hard on me as well as many others in the company.

The rugged travel took its toll on one's appearance. In those days people bathed and changed clothing only about once a week under normal circumstances, and under trail conditions it was even less often. The trail was especially rough on long skirts. As the women and girls stumbled over rocks and through brush, their dresses snagged on branches, tearing off pieces of cloth. Fanny Fry, age sixteen, had walked over one thousand miles in 1859 on bare, swollen feet when she entered Salt Lake City:

A nice picture I looked, I can assure you: an old sunbonnet on my head all torn, an old jacket, and my petticoat tattered, and my feet dressed in rags. . . . I went the entire trip without shoes.

Clothes were important to girls then, as they are now. Martha Ann Morrison could still remember years later the embarrassment she felt wearing her ragged dress, which barely covered her body by the time she arrived in Oregon in 1844, at age thirteen. The last leg of the trip, trudging through the swamp to get to their land claim, was a final humiliation:

We had to wade through the tremendous swamps. I knew some of the young men that were along laughed at us girls for holding up what dresses we had to keep from miring, but we did not think it was funny. We finally waded through.

Camp Life

About the only time the emigrants had to rest, socialize, and enjoy themselves was when they stopped to camp. Many journals and memoirs rendered camp scenes with great fondness. James Brown, the captain of an 1854 Mormon company, painted a lively picture of a typical camp:

All is life and activity when cooking, washing, watching, singing, talking, laughing, and little girls and boys running, jumping, and skipping about camp. It is truly a great work and a wonder.

There was a lot to be done in setting up camp for the night, and everyone helped. Men usually unyoked the animals and pitched the tents, children gathered fuel for the fires, women made the fires and prepared the food. Most companies also dug a latrine ditch. The unwritten rule was "Ladies on the left, gents on the right." Women and girls used their long skirts as a privacy screen.

Cooking was generally done over an open fire of wood, sagebrush, or, most commonly, dried buffalo manure (which didn't really smell that bad). Camp food consisted mostly of beans, rice, bacon, dried meat (jerky), and biscuits or sourdough bread, along with occasional dried fruits. Most emigrants had cows, so there was usually milk and butter. At times someone might catch some fish or shoot some game, and the company would feast on grizzly bear soup or roast antelope, sage hen, or rabbit. In season they could sometimes find wild berries, a true delicacy. William M. Colvig, who was just six in 1851, had fond memories of camp food:

I can still visualize our family wagon [and] the smell of the smoke
of our campfire [and] the delicious odor of frying antelope steak
mingled with the fragrant aroma of coffee or sizzling bacon.

After supper and chores, evenings were a time to relax. Helen
Stewart portrays a cozy scene in her diary in 1853:

The children is grumbling and crying and laughing and hollering
and playing all round while I am in the tent. . . . Little Byron is
lying beside me enjoying sweet repose.

Families usually slept in the wagons or in tents. If there weren't
enough tents to go around, the young men and sometimes the older
ones, too, slept on the ground under the wagons or out in the open.

Camping wasn't "roughing it" for everyone. Sallie Hester revealed
how well supplied the wagons in her company were in 1849. Sallie's
father was a successful lawyer, and they had a carriage, a sign of wealth:

May 21, Sunday. . . . We have a cooking stove made of sheet iron, a
portable table, tin plates and cups, cheap knives and forks (best
ones packed away), camp stools, etc. We sleep in our wagons on
feather beds; the men who drive for us in the tent. We live on
bacon, ham, rice, dried fruits, molasses, packed butter, bread, cof-
fee, tea and milk as we have our own cows. Occasionaly the men
kill an antelope and then we have a feast; and sometimes we
have fish on Sunday.

As darkness fell, under ideal conditions all would be peaceful.
Sara Alexander, nineteen-year-old pioneer of 1859, left a vivid picture of what evenings were like along much of the trail:

The vast, open surroundings was forced upon the consciousness;
the stillness, the vastness, the night with the moon and stars shining
over us was all so overwhelming in its beauty and greatness that a
heathen must have been impressed with the presence of a God.

Charley True, who took his turn standing guard over the herds at night as a sixteen-year-old in 1859, also gave a lyrical description of nighttime on the plains:

The moonlight cast an eerie light over the prairies. As I stood my solitary watch, I remember feeling almost overwhelmed by the vast loneliness of my position—a boy alone in the midst of a vast wilderness. . . . I stood watch alone with the unearthly howls of the coyotes breaking the silence, and I remember feeling an intense awareness of the beauty of the moonlit landscape and the wonder of my being there.

Perhaps as he stood there Charley pondered the vast Milky Way and tried to count some of the 400 million stars in our galaxy. That starry prairie sky must have glittered more brightly than any of the nightscapes most modern Americans can see.

At daybreak, camps moved to a rhythm of routine, building fires, milking cows, and having breakfast, then breaking down the camp and gathering the livestock. In 1842 company leader Dr. Elijah White depicted a typical scene:

As day dawned . . . the boys went out in all directions to collect the teams and herds, which often detailed them for several hours, as the cattle would sometimes wander off for miles.

They usually moved out about 7 A.M. Most every wagon in the company tried to be the first to leave each morning. Those in the rear would have to eat a lot of dust. They had many miles to cover before they would stop again.

Lighter Loads, Heavier Hearts

To lighten heavy wagons, the pioneers often had to discard personal items a few hundred miles along the route. When the trail got hilly, sandy, or rocky, teams faltered and wagons broke down. Out went stoves, mirrors, chests, beds, rocking chairs, barrels, farming equipment, dishes, and musical instruments. Eventually they dumped even clothing and food to ease the load of weary oxen. Abandoned items littered the trail for miles.

As the emigrants approached the mountains, the trail became one vast flea market. Near Fort Laramie, in present eastern Wyoming, one could find almost anything, even entire wagons. Emigrants often left belongings at the fort, hoping to come back for them later. According to one historian, a company from St. Louis dumped out a ton of cured meat and a wagonload of bacon near Fort Laramie in 1849. Another wagon train poured barrels of whiskey in a stream and wondered what it would do to the fish. Books by the hundreds lay strewn about. Many emigrants were appalled at all the waste and picked up some of the treasures, only to have their captain order that the items be thrown out that evening.

All along the trail, even near the end, emigrants had to relinquish cherished possessions. One man in Lucy Henderson's company in 1846 pleaded to keep his mother's rolling pin, which he had protected all the way from Missouri, but it was tossed. "I shall never forget how that big man stood there with tears streaming down his face," Lucy, age eleven at the time, later wrote. Tears did not move the captains, for there was little room for sentiment on the trail when it was a matter of life or death.

Mary Williamson, age fifteen, was torn between duty and personal attachment in 1856 when the captain of her handcart company asked her to throw out her favorite keepsake, a small lion made of iron. Mary pleaded to keep her treasure, but the captain refused. She could not bear to watch as it was tossed on the pile of discards. That night, when the others in camp were asleep, Mary crept back to the pile. She grabbed her lion, tied it with a string, and put it underneath her dress. Mary and her keepsake survived the journey, but the lion left a permanent imprint on the girl's body that was visible for the rest of her life.

Sixteen-year-old Bernard White's family, caught in a snowstorm on their way to Utah in 1856, buried many valuable articles near Devil's Gate in central Wyoming, hoping to return for them later. Among the items were heirloom china and a silver tea set. "We only saved one ox and one cow of our team. We were disabled and left our wagon and all our trunks and baggage," Bernard recalled. He did not mention whether the family got their things back. Most pioneers never retrieved cached belongings.

Seeing the Elephant

"Seeing the elephant" was an expression pioneers used for the hardships, mishaps, illnesses, and traumas of the trail. It became part of trail lore to mention seeing the elephant, and events were often exaggerated. Many however, saw much worse than an "elephant," and some lost their lives. (You will read about these more serious episodes in a later chapter.) But even the luckiest did not traverse the overland trail without suffering a little.

In 1852 Mrs. Eliza Brooks and her six children, all under thirteen, started for California to meet Mr. Brooks, who was already there. Mrs. Brooks hired a teamster to drive the oxen, but he lost his courage at Council Bluffs, Iowa. Her son Elisha Brooks, eleven at the time, remembered the episode about seventy years later:

The air was thick . . . with tales of Indian massacres, starvation and pestilence. It required stout hearts to stem this gloomy regurgitating tide. Our company quailed before it and went to pieces, some settling there and some returning home. Our teamster, as fainthearted as the rest, deserted us in spite of Mother's earnest pleading; and there we were stranded on the swollen Missouri.

Mrs. Brooks asked the children what they wanted to do, and they all agreed to go ahead:

After a week's delay . . . in waiting for the flood to subside, she crossed the river and pushed out into the mysterious West, into the teeth of the unknown terrors—alone with her six little children.

This family saw more of the elephant on their journey, but they were all alive when their father met them in California that fall.

It was not uncommon for teamsters to prove unreliable. Many young men eager to get to the goldfields out west signed up as teamsters in exchange for board. But it did not always work out. Some teamsters were evicted from Wilford Woodruff's Mormon company in 1850. A young woman with that company, Miss Sophia Goodridge, wrote of the incident in her diary:

> We were detained in the morning until nearly noon on account of Brother Woodruff's teamsters. One of them was fired and the other two left. They were rough, obscene men, did not belong to the church and were stealing the supplies.

Seventeen-year-old Abigail Scott's family also had teamster problems, in 1852:

> Owning to the carelessness of one of the drivers the wagon in which myself and sisters were riding ran into a deep mud hole and upset; We were very much frightened. The wagon contained chests of clothing and feather beds. . . . The wagon bows were all broken. After having been told to leave the train or do better [the driver] took French leave of us, and we have not seen or heard of him since.

The trail brought out the best and worst in human nature. Sometimes tempers flared over simple incidents, and fighting often broke out. Mr. James Godfrey, a teamster from Alton, Illinois, en route to California, had a firsthand encounter with cantankerous trail companions on July 22, 1850:

> We had rather an unpleasant altercation in camp this evening in which one man raised an axe to another; no harm was done however, one being afraid and the other dared not strike. Both were soon heartily ashamed of it. The boys have humorously styled it: "The Battle of the Humboldt," and the two poor fellows will not hear the last of it as long as we are together.

Not all feuds ended so amicably. Sometimes there was bloodshed.

It was not just human foibles that the emigrants had to contend with on the trail. Nature could be an even more powerful enemy. Mary Elizabeth Munkers recalled a fierce Nebraska rainstorm in 1846, when she was ten:

> I remember while we were camped on the Platte the whole sky became black as ink. A terrific wind came up, which blew the covers off the wagons and blew down the tents. When the storm burst upon us it frightened the cattle, so it took all the efforts of the men to keep them from stampeding. It seemed as if the sky was a huge lake or an ocean and [was] slopping over.... The men had to chain the wagons together to keep them from being blown in the river.

While some places had too much moisture, others had too little. The arid climate of what is now Nevada was especially harsh for the pioneers. Charley True remembered suffering there in 1859:

> At this time we were on a rocky dusty road not far from the sink of the Humboldt, which we could see some distance in advance. After several weeks of exposure, our distress from chapped faces and hands had now reached an acute stage. The alkaline dust and water acted like a solution of caustic, and the slightest friction caused the blood to flow from the cracks of our faces and hands.

Nature also bombarded the emigrants with terrible pests, especially mosquitos. One diarist mentioned swallowing "mouth fulls of mosquitoes" on the trip. Another pioneer wrote that the small children had been bitten so much they "looked like they had measles." Still another remarked that the mosquitos could "sting through a copper kettle." The emigrants were also plagued by chiggers, fleas, flies, gnats, ticks, lice, ants, bedbugs, grasshoppers, scorpions, and spiders. But it was the mosquitos they complained about most. Mr. Elisha Douglass Perkins described the misery caused by these nasty critters in 1849:

Never in my life did I have the misfortune to fall into the hands of such a . . . merciless set & they came in such perfect clouds & their sting was so sharp . . . that sleep was out of the question.

The Good Times

The pioneers were a hardy lot whose spirits were seldom defeated by any kind of elephant. After overcoming difficult obstacles, they often celebrated. Mr. Henry Lienhard captured a scene of frivolity after his group survived the Nevada desert in 1846:

The young girls danced together and sang. Everybody was in good spirits. Stories were told, and there was singing and dancing. . . . The young girls . . . danced till the dust flew.

There was indeed much joy on the journey in spite of the hardships. The trail offered young pioneers many unique positive experiences. No one "back in the states" could see snow in July and August. On high mountain passes, one might hold wildflowers in one hand and a snowball in the other. Youngsters could even enjoy "Sweetwater ice cream" (snow mixed with sugar and milk or cream) made with the mountain snow.

Romania Bunnell, age fifteen in 1855, remembered her overland trek with delight:

The journey across the plains with ox teams was a summer full of pleasure to me; the early morning walks gathering wild flowers, climbing the rugged and ofttimes forbidding hills—the pleasant evenings by the bright camp fire, while sweet songs floated forth . . . gladdened our young hearts.

A later chapter discusses in detail some of the other fun and celebratory experiences the emigrants had.

Famous Landmarks

The many landmarks along the overland trails were very important to the pioneers, not merely as scenery but as milestones to mark their progress. Some of these places were legendary natural wonders, such as Chimney Rock, and Devil's Gate. Many emigrants had expectations based on what they had heard about these famous spots, so they were often surprised at what they actually found when they got there. Children especially took some of the poetic names literally. As Charley True remembered of Devil's Gate in present Wyoming: "I so well recall my disappointment at finding no gate. There might have been some devils near, but as to a Devil's Gate—I saw none."

Many of these scenic wonders inspired awe in the pioneers who viewed them. Others were simply a novelty. Passing emigrants marked Chimney Rock and Independence Rock with nineteenth-century graffiti, some of which is still there today. At times

Chimney Rock.
—Author photo

the landmarks could even prove dangerous. A few people died and others were injured while trying to scale Devil's Gate and Independence Rock.

Chimney Rock, in present Nebraska, is a stunning, funnel-shaped, clay-and-sandstone pillar rising five hundred feet above the Platte River. It was the first major landmark on the trail. A few miles farther west was the massive cliff called Scotts Bluff. Continuing westward into what is now Wyoming, the weary travelers were much relieved to reach their next landmark, Fort Laramie. The military posts along the trail offered a rare opportunity to freshen up, make repairs, and restock supplies. Sallie Hester mentioned stopping at the fort in her diary in 1849:

Fort Laramie, June 19. This fort is of adobe, enclosed with a high wall of the same. The entrance is a hole in the wall just large enough for a person to crawl through. Men were engaged in all kinds of business from blacksmith up. [We] enjoyed it to the fullest extent after our long tramp.

Scotts Bluff, with wagon replicas.
—Author photo

About one hundred miles ride past Fort Laramie the emigrants had to traverse a fifty-mile stretch of alkali, sand, sagebrush, and mud known as "Hell's Reach" before arriving at the Sweetwater River and Independence Rock in central Wyoming. After trudging over this rough terrain, reaching the Sweetwater was a cause for celebration.

Independence Rock was an intriguing spot. This dome-shaped, mostly granite rock is about 190 feet high and half a mile long. Catholic missionary Pierre-Jean De Smet dubbed it the "Register of the Desert" because so many pioneers signed their name on it when they reached it.

It was difficult to carve into the hard granite, so most emigrants painted their names, sometimes using odd mixtures that may have included gunpowder, tar, or buffalo fat. Sallie Hester carved her signature on the rock rather than painting it, which took a long time: "July 2 passed Independence Rock. This rock is covered with names. With great difficulty I found a place to cut mine."

Along with adding their own names to the "register," young pioneers often looked for the signatures of others. It was a thrill to find a familiar name there. "Can you imagine our joy on finding our father's name among the rest, placed there two years before. Our names are now there," Elisha Brooks recalled.

Although Charley True apparently did not leave his name on the rock, he was impressed with the names he saw:

There were hundreds and hundreds of names done in lamp-black and oil, axle grease, paint—anything that could be daubed on. . . . Each one seemed to have tried to outdo the other in placing his name in the most conspicuously high position. We wondered in many cases what method had been adopted to place names far above others, thus gaining greater publicity. . . . It was here we found the names of J. C. Fremont, Brigham Young, Kit Carson and many others prominent in helping blaze the trails of these western wilds.

A short ride past Independence Rock was Devil's Gate, a dramatic cleft in the long craggy hillside. Like Independence Rock, Devil's Gate was surrounded with lore, including tragic true stories of people who tried and failed to scale its rocky walls. A spectacular view rewarded those who did make it to the top, but sometimes the climb was more than one bargained for, as eighteen-year-old John Steele and his friends found out in 1850:

Creeping cautiously up and clinging to the projecting points, we ascended about three hundred feet [then] a furious hailstorm swept down the river, and for two hours, we lay upon the rocks's smooth surface, and pressed our fingers into the crevice to prevent being blown off. . . . The wind howled through the canon, hurling pebbles, branches and dust into the air, smearing us with mud, while rain and hail beat in upon us in merciless glee; we kept a death-like grip on the rocks.

The young men all finally made it down safely.

South Pass through the Rocky Mountains, at the Continental Divide in present Wyoming, lay about one hundred miles west of Devil's Gate. Arriving at the pass was another milestone of the journey. Judging by these comments from Charley True, the scenery was awesome:

Our ascent to South Pass was very gradual. We could scarcely realize that we were at last standing on the very apex of the Rocky Mountains—the Continental Divide of North America. To our surprise there were no trees, no crags, no peaks, and no evidences of any violent paroxysms of nature either of ancient or modern times. A most wonderful panorama, however, of vast dome-like mountains encircled us. Magnificent vistas stretched away as far as the eye could reach. We stood enraptured.

Twenty miles beyond South Pass, the trails separated. Some emigrants eventually turned north to Oregon as others continued southwest to Utah and beyond.

The California Trail

Those en route to California faced some of the most difficult terrain in the West, including a scorching desert and the towering Sierra Nevada. At first they followed the Humboldt River, also known as the "Humbug River." The water was fine at the head of the river, but eventually it began to thin out, meander, and smell bad. Still, it went in the right direction, and a bad river is better than no river.

Along the Humboldt were two major hot springs, which afforded some convenient culinary shortcuts. In 1847 Mr. Henry William Bigler noted: "Aug 14, camped at boiling springs. . . . Here we made our tea and coffee without fire to heat the water." These springs could be dangerous, however. People and animals were often scalded—sometimes to death—when they fell or jumped into them.

Past the Humboldt, California-bound travelers had to cross the dreaded Forty Mile Desert. Elizabeth Keegan wrote a letter to her two siblings in St. Louis describing their troubles crossing this desert in 1852:

> Many teams go in on this desert but few come out of it. The mules we had [pulling] our carriage gave out. . . . We had great difficulty. . . . When we got across we laid up for a week and sent back for the carriage.

Just when these pioneers were the most exhausted, they met their biggest challenge—crossing the steep, craggy mountains known as the Sierra Nevada. After struggling forty miles in the desert, the emigrants had to summon their last ounce of energy, courage, and determination as the Sierras loomed resplendent and unbelievably daunting.

Amazingly, the difficulty of the task before them did not dampen the enthusiasm of the young pioneers. Perhaps because they were at last so close to their destination, they often met the challenge with great joy. Eliza Ann McAuley reveals her optimistic spirit:

*September 14th, 1852. We climbed the highest peaks near the road,
and were well repaid for our trouble by the splendid view. On one
side the snow-capped peaks rise in majestic grandeur, on the other
they are covered to their summit with tall pine and fir, while
before us in the top of the mountains, apparently an old crater, lies
a beautiful lake [Lake Tahoe] in which the Truckee takes its rise.
. . . We vented our patriotism by singing "The Star Spangled Banner" and afterward enjoyed a merry game of snow-ball.*

Over the Sierras was a beautiful meadow with water and grass.
The destination, Sutter's Fort in California, was only about one
hundred miles from this spot.

The Road to Oregon

While the California-bound plodded through the desert and
scaled the Sierras, those on the Oregon Trail had their own obstacles to surmount. Crossing the Columbia River was especially
fraught with danger. The Jesse Applegate party in 1843 had reason
to remember this part of the journey because three children
drowned.

Abigail Scott and her family had to cross the Deschutes River, a
tributary of the Columbia, in 1852:

*Early this morning we took up our line of march and came to the
Deshutes . . . a rapid, turbid stream. We got an Indian to pilot the
wagons across the river. . . . After getting all safely over we ascended a long, steep and rocky hill, when we again overlooked the
Columbia river adorned on each bank with lofty bluffs of basaltic
rock. . . . Mts Hood & St. Heleens were also in plain view.*

The Scott family took the Barlow Road through the Cascade
Mountains. The Barlow Road was completed in the summer of
1846 to allow better and easier passage into the Willamette Valley.
It was the best way into Oregon City. When the Scotts arrived, it

The end of the Oregon Trail, Oregon City. —Author photo

was still barely a path in the forest. Two men guarded the toll gate and charged five dollars on each wagon and ten cents per animal. Five dollars was the equivalent of about fifty dollars today. Going to Oregon was not a cheap adventure.

The Barlow route was rough but impressive. Pine, oak, and fir trees, as well as rhododendrons, lined the road. Mary Dunn also took this route in 1852, when she was sixteen:

> We had a pretty hard time at what they called the Devil's Backbone, now known as Laurel Hill. When we came to the Dalles, 48 of our wagons went down the Columbia, but 12 wagons, including our own, decided to come by the Barlow Road. They rough-locked the wheels, cut a tree down to drag back of the wagons to serve as a brake, and let one yoke of oxen go ahead to pull the wagon down the hill.

Most emigrants agreed that Laurel Hill was the major obstacle of the route. Still, they moved ahead with determination and their last reserves of energy, urging weary animals—and one another—forward yard by yard, mile after mile. Wasn't paradise just around the corner?

—SUMMARY—

During their months on the trail, the young pioneers faced difficult terrain, bad weather, and physical pain; they made many personal sacrifices and often had little food to sustain them. Yet despite the hardships, these valiant youngsters persevered. In fact, most young emigrants enjoyed their journey and thrived in later years. The pitfalls seemed to pale in comparison to the delights of laughing around a campfire, signing Independence Rock, picking mountain wildflowers, eating a fresh antelope steak or some Sweetwater ice cream, and singing "The Star Spangled Banner" from the summit of the Sierra Nevada. Perhaps "seeing the elephant" was not such a bad way to start life!

Profile of
MOSES SHALLENBERGER

On November 9, 1826, in Stark County, Ohio, a little boy was born to a Swiss couple, Jacob and Barbara Shallenberger. They called him Moses. He was the youngest of twelve children, seven of whom survived into adulthood. Eighteen years later and two thousand miles away, Moses would make history.

After Moses's parents died, he went to live with his sister Elizabeth and her husband, John Townsend, in Missouri. In 1843 Townsend, a physician and merchant, got the fever to migrate west. The next spring he packed his wagon with a supply of silks and other materials, as well as some books, and headed to the Overland Trail starting point at Council Bluffs, Iowa, with his wife and young brother-in-law.

Moses was one of forty-six people in about forty wagons who gathered at the banks of the Missouri River in mid-May 1844. Most were headed to California. Moses helped get some scared, stubborn cattle across the river, but watched helplessly as other animals drowned in a sea of mud. It was only the beginning of his adventure. Chosen "a corporal of the guard" with his friend John Murphy, Moses moved out with the rest on the Great North Platte River Road.

Later that fall in the Sierra Nevada, Moses and two other young men volunteered to guard some of the wagons while the rest of the company moved ahead. Over the next two days, the three young men built a log cabin, roofed with hides and pine boughs. Inside they set up a stone fireplace. Moses later wrote:

> On the evening of the day we finished our little house it began to snow, and fell to a depth of three feet. This prevented a hunt which we had in contemplation for the next day.

The deep snow worried the young men. They decided to push ahead and join the others, through snow that was now about fifteen feet deep. But Moses got sick and had to turn back:

> The feelings that came over me I cannot express. . . . I strapped on my blankets and dried beef, shouldered my gun, and began to retrace my steps. . . . It had frozen during the night and [I could] walk on our trail without snow-shoes. I think I was never so tired in my life as when just a little before dark, I came in sight of the cabin.

Moses set some traps he found and went to bed.

As soon as daylight came I was out to inspect the traps. I was anxious to see them and still I dreaded to look. After some hesitation I commenced, and to my great delight I found in one of them a starved coyote.

Moses did not relish the bony critter, but it was edible. Better food was not to be had: the deer had gone to lower elevations and the bears were hibernating. Moses survived the winter on crows, coyotes, and foxes.

My life was more miserable than I can describe. . . . I was always worried, not about myself alone, but in regard to the fate of those who had gone forward.

Luckily, Moses had the books his sister's husband had brought in the wagon. His favorite was a volume of Lord Byron's poetry. Reading was one way to stave off his loneliness:

I used to often read aloud for I longed for some sound to break the oppressive stillness. For the same reason, I would talk aloud to myself. At night I built large fires and read by the light of the pine knots as late as possible, in order that I might sleep late the next morning, and thus cause the days to seem shorter.

In February he got a joyful surprise:

One evening, a little before sunset, about the last of February, as I was standing a short distance from my cabin. . . . I thought I could distinguish the form of a man moving towards me. . . . Very soon I recognized the familiar face of Dennis Martin.

Moses made it safely back to Sutter's Fort in California, where he rejoined his party. He lived with his sister and brother-in-law until he regained his strength. They both died a few years later, and Moses took care of their young child in California.

The cabin Moses built in the Sierras was later used by the Reed family of the ill-fated Donner-Reed party. In 1995 the Nevada County Historical Commission and the California Department of Parks and Recreation dedicated a plaque to Moses. Thirty miles west of present-day Reno, Nevada, it sits a few yards from the Pioneer Monument, which tells about the Donner-Reed tragedy. The inscription to Moses reads, in part:

> Near this spot stood a small cabin built by 18-year-old Moses Schallenberger and two other men. They were members of the Stevens-Townsend-Murphy Party of 1844, the first pioneers to take wagons over the Sierra Nevada, opening the Truckee Route of the California Trail. . . .
>
> The courage and resolution of Moses Schallenberger during his solitary winter ordeal in this cabin makes him one of the true heroes in the saga of the California Trail.

Moses married Sanny Everitt, a teacher, in 1854. They lived in San Jose, California, and had five children. Moses dictated his memoirs to his daughter in 1884, forty years after he was on the trail.

THREE

Fun and Recreation

*We had a great dance tonight. ag [her sister, Agnes] and I
went up on the hill and talked over old times . . . and then
we came down and danced until neerly one oclock. It done
very well for want of better fun. It is a beautiful eavening
the stars shine bright.*

—Diary of Helen Stewart, age seventeen, 1853

Children on the Overland Trail had little in the way of entertainment media, playthings, or recreational opportunities. These
youngsters, however, had none of the expectations we have today
and found amusement wherever they could. For fun they explored
the landscape, had footraces and horse races, and made up their
own games. Mrs. Ruth Shackleford, on the trail in 1865, noted,
"The girls made a swing and enjoyed themselves for awhile."

Sometimes sheer silliness erupted out of nowhere. Rhoda Quick,
age seven at the time, recalled this scene in 1852:

*I remember when we were coming through Iowa, we stopped and
asked two girls we met what county we were in. One of them dug
her bare toes in the mud by the roadside, and pushing back her
sunbonnet, drawled, "You are in Pottawatomie County, Iowa." That*

was too much for us children. We went off like a bunch of fire-crackers. It doesn't take much to amuse a bunch of children.

Mother Nature sometimes provided entertainment. Youngsters chased after fireflies, butterflies, and grasshoppers: "We saw a great variety of brilliantly coloured grasshoppers, some being very large. . . . The children hunted them with great glee," Mr. Frederick Piercy wrote in 1853.

Occasionally children got a little carried away in finding amusements. Jesse Applegate and his playmates made up a game involving a dead ox in 1843, when he was seven, which he wrote about years later:

The sport consisted in running and butting the head against the paunch [of the dead ox] and being bounced back, the recoil being in proportion to the force of the contact. One of the boys [misjudged the target and] charged the paunch at the top of his speed, and within a couple of yards of the target came down like a pile driver against the paunch, but did not bound back. . . . We took hold of his legs and pulled him out.

Water Recreation

Water has always offered opportunities for recreation. Swimming was a popular pastime when there was water nearby. But it was never a coed sport. Girls usually had an adult woman along to supervise. Boys swam on their own, and more often, usually in the nude. Interestingly, only boys "went swimming" in those days; women and girls "went in bathing." Helen Stewart, showing a budding frontier feminism, once joined the boys along the Platte River in 1853:

June 9. We started early this morning, oh it is extremely hot. . . . We have stopt to eat dinner. Five of the boys are in swimming. I wish I could go to, so I do.

The Platte River in Wyoming. —Author photo

The Platte was the most popular river for swimming. Mary Ann Stearns, nineteen, and some other young women in her company in 1852 enjoyed a midnight dip in that river:

> *There was one thing we enjoyed very much, and that was the bath in the river. . . . [We] procured a bathing suit of some kind, and we took our baths by starlight.*

Seventeen-year-old Welborn Beeson was a master swimmer, going to Grand Island in the middle of the Platte, about a quarter of a mile each way, in 1853: "May 21. Been the hottest day we have had yet this year. I swam over to Grand Island this afternoon."

Ruth May, age thirteen in 1867, captured the sense of appreciation at finding water on the long, hot trail:

> *No one but those who have walked over prairies and deserts for days, where water is so scarce that the creeks were reduced to little puddles of alkali water, can imagine the beauty and glory of a river! On the Sweetwater we rested, washed our clothing, went in bathing, and had a real jollification.*

Fishing was another favorite activity when the pioneers were near water. Miss Sophia Goodridge and her teenage brother George had success on the Green River in Wyoming in 1850: "Sept 23. George caught a cat fish a foot long. We spent the day fishing. Caught some beautiful large trout."

Both boys and girls commonly fished. Helen Stewart and her sister Agnes threw a line in on several occasions, but Helen didn't seem to get much out of it:

> I neather like to put the grass hopper on, nor take the fish [off], poor things. We all went fishing this eavening there was 11 in number of us I believe they all caught some thing, me I got two little wee things that was not worth ceaping and threw them in to the water again.

Toys and Games

Emigrant children's toys were simple and few. Though a child might be allowed to bring a single treasured toy on the journey, most such things had to be left behind. Therefore many playthings on the frontier were homemade. Something as simple as a rock, a stick, or even a buffalo chip might suffice as a toy or game piece.

Most girls played with dolls in those days, as they have from time immemorial. Few pioneer girls had store-bought dolls, but many had homemade rag dolls and sometimes stick dolls. These could be as simple or elaborate as one's time, money, and talents permitted. One trail mother stayed up all night to make her daughter a doll, then woke her up early to see "her look of utter joy." Alma Mineer, age six in 1861, later remembered her sisters making dolls: "My older sisters used to make rag dolls as they walked along for us little children to play with."

Games, too, were simple, requiring only minimal accessories, if any. Games children played on the trail included I-spy, hunt-the-thimble, hide-and-seek, ring-around-the-rosey, red rover, leapfrog, blindman's bluff, jump rope, marbles, and various ball games. They also played sitting games such as checkers, dominos, and cards. Many of the games they played are still around today.

Many Victorian-era teenagers played a board game called Mansions of Happiness. Published by S. B. Ives in 1843, it taught moral values such as piety, chastity, and temperance. It was the first popular board game in America. Seventeen-year-old Frances Ward played this game en route to California from Wisconsin. Her mother noted Frankie's game in her diary:

> June 16, 1853. Frank and a number of young friends are amusing themselves with the 'Mansions of Happiness,' and judging from their merry laugh, I should think they were enjoying it very much indeed.

Another game some young emigrants played was chess. Mary Eliza Warner, fifteen, wrote in her 1864 diary, "Aunt Celia and I played Chess which Mrs. Lord thought was the first step toward gambling."

Risky Business

Sometimes "fun" had the potential for disaster. A popular game at the time was mumblety-peg, which involved throwing an open-bladed knife to make it stick into the ground. Aurelia Spencer and her siblings engaged in this dangerous activity while camped at Winter Quarters, Nebraska, in the winter of 1846–47, when she was twelve:

> When the weather was cold or stormy and we could not go out, the game of mumble-peg was introduced which was all the rage among the children at that time. This we used to play on our dirt floor, which rather marred its smoothness but afforded us considerable amusement.

Guns, too, were commonly used for recreation. Since most youngsters, especially boys, learned to handle a gun at an early age, target shooting was one of the most attractive amusements on the trail. Welborn Beeson mentions this activity in 1853: "April 2. We had a little shooting match. Jim Logan made the best shot." Though target shooting was potentially dangerous, parents did not discourage it because it helped hone an essential survival skill.

Young people sometimes got into trouble in pursuit of less worthy pleasures, however. What started out as a little experimentation ended up a near-death experience for Barnet Simpson, age nine in 1846. His first encounter with a homemade brew called "white lightning" afterward turned him into a sworn teetotaler:

> *My father told me to look up a bridle that had been mislaid, so John [his uncle], and I started to look for it. While looking under one of the wagons John saw a stone jug. . . . John said: "This is whiskey, Did you ever drink any corn liquor, Barnet?" My father was a Primitive Baptist preacher and was very strict, so I had never tasted liquor. . . . John thought it would be funny if he could get me drunk, so he suggested that we drink some whiskey. By 5 o'clock I couldn't walk [and] I fell in a stupor and foamed at the mouth and had convulsions. They thought I was going to die. . . . I never tasted liquor of any kind again.*

Campfire Evenings

In the evenings, after the emigrants had made camp and eaten supper, they usually tried to relax a bit before going to bed. Families would often sit around the campfire and joke, sing, and tell stories. Abigail Scott, seventeen, wrote about a typical evening on July 9, 1852:

> *We have a fair specimen here tonight of the various occupations of different persons in the [camp]. Betting and playing cards is going on at one encampment, music and dancing at another, while at a third persons are engaged singing religious hymns and psalms with apparent devotion.*

Camp scenes such as the one seventeen-year-old Eliza Ann McAuley described in her diary in 1852 became some of the fondest memories of the journey:

> *There are a great many camped here and a merrier set I never saw. Just after dark we were treated to a variety of barnyard music in various parts of the camp. Roosters crowed, hens cackled, ducks quacked, pigs squealed, owls hooted, donkeys brayed, dogs howled, cats squalled and all this perfect imitations were made by human voices.*

When things were quiet, books were a very important source of enjoyment for the pioneers. They read mostly in the evenings, by lantern light. Though many wagon parties had to throw out their books to make room for provisions, the lucky ones were able to keep a few. This meant that youngsters' choices in books were very limited, so they often read advanced material, such as *Paradise Lost* and *Pilgrim's Progress,* which most young people today would not encounter until college. If nothing else, most every emigrant family had a Bible, the most frequently read book on the trail for adults and children alike.

Edible Treats

Modern parents commonly give their children sweets every day, but this was not the case in the nineteenth century. Because supplies were limited, sugar was a premium item on the trail. This meant that candy and cookies were a dramatic change from the usual camp fare. Eliza Ann McAuley and her sister Margaret enjoyed these rare treats while camping on the Bear River in 1852:

> *The cattle [are] wading in wild oats up to their eyes while we have fun making pop corn candy. Margaret is baking cookies, but the boys steal them as fast as she can bake them.*

59

Kate McDaniel, age eight when she traveled the California Trail from Illinois in 1853, remembered her mother's animal-shaped cookies:

Mother had been artist enough in cutting them out, that we could pick out the different shapes. We cherished our little cookies & were loath to eat them. But finally we could not resist the temptation to take just a wee taste; so few sweets did we get those days. . . . We would take a bite and nibble like mice. We would try to make them last as long as possible.

Margaret Judd, age seventeen, had picked some wild berries on the trail one day and decided to display her culinary skills and impress the young men with a "pie party" in 1849:

There were several nice young men in our company, which made it interesting for the girls. . . . I asked some of the girls and boys to come to a reception one evening after the chores were done. . . . Pies were a great luxury and seldom seen on the plains.

Margaret's pies were not such a luxury, however. Everyone ate them without comment because people were very polite in those days. Later Margaret tasted the pies herself:

Oh, my, how it set my teeth on edge. . . . That ended my pie making on the plains. . . . I don't think there was enough sugar in camp to have sweetened those pies.

Music, Singing, and Dancing

Singing was a favorite pastime, as it required nothing but a voice to participate. Some of the most enthusiastic comments in pioneer diaries had to do with music and singing. Mr. Elisha Douglass Perkins, en route to California in 1849, got a chance to admire a pretty girl with a guitar from St. Louis:

I saw a Doctors family in a large spring carriage. . . . Miss Fanny, his oldest looked Entirely out of the proper place amid these rough scenes though she appears to enjoy herself much. she has her guitar with her & sings & plays very finely & seems to care little whether she is in her parlour at home or sitting on a sand bank on the Humboldt, so long as she can make music.

Sallie Hester, age fourteen, noted with sadness the departure of some amiable musical companions in 1849:

This week some of our company left us, all young men. They were jolly, merry fellows and gave life to our lonely evenings. We all miss them very much. some had violins, others guitars, and some had fine voices, and they always had a good audience.

The handcart companies often sang as they traveled, for it made the time pass more pleasantly. They loved to sing the songs of Zion as they marched along, especially *The Handcart Song:*

> *Ye Saints that Dwell on Europe's shores,*
> *Prepare yourselves with many more*
> *To leave behind your native land*
> *For sure God's Judgments are at hand*
> *Prepare to cross the stormy main*
> *Before you do the valley gain*
> *And with the faithful make a start*
> *To cross the plains with your handcart.*

> Chorus
> *Some must push and some must pull*
> *As we go marching up the hill,*
> *As merrily on the way we go*
> *Until we reach the valley, Oh.*

Another musical activity, dancing, was a delightful diversion for young pioneers. Square dancing was one of the most popular dances of the mid-1800s, and "Bow to your partner and do-si-do" could be heard at night in some camps when weather and time allowed. Mormons permitted most kinds of dancing except the daring waltz, which had recently come into vogue. However, emigrants of some other religions, such as strict Baptists, thought dancing was a great sin, and they were shocked that the Mormons permitted this activity.

Some diaries mention dancing on top of Independence Rock in central Wyoming, which must have been a romantic and thrilling experience for those energetic enough to get up there. Sixteen-year-old Martin Luther Ensign described having such an frolic with other young people in 1847:

> Went to Independence Rock on the Sweetwater River. Camped here and had a dance on the rock, it being flat on top and large enough for a cotillion.

The Big Celebration

Everyone wanted to make it to Independence Rock for the Fourth of July, the big day to celebrate on the trail. Whether they made it to the rock or not, emigrants nearly always had a party on Independence Day. Everyone sang songs and waved flags, which were often homemade. The men read the Declaration of Independence, made speeches, and fired off guns while the women performed culinary miracles in the desert. They saved their best food for this occasion. Some emigrants had canned oysters and sardines, powdered lemonade, and fruitcake. Virginia Reed, age twelve, wrote her cousin on July 4, 1846:

> My Dear Cousin. . . . We selabrated the 4 of July on plat [Platte River] at bever criek. Pa treted the company and we all had some leminade. . . . We are all doing Well and in hye sperits.

Eighteen-year-old John Steele noted his camp's grand and patriotic festivities in 1850:

Thursday, July 4. Last night the boys of our camp made arrangements for celebrating Independence Day. About 3 P.M. we reached Sweetwater River and camped near Independence Rock. . . . About ten in the evening camp fires were replenished and there arose a shout that rolled from camp to camp until it died out in the distance . . . followed by the discharge of fire arms, which closed the celebration.

Helen Stewart, seventeen, felt she was missing out on the fun in 1853: "This is the fourth in the States. . . . All is prepareing for

The Sweetwater River with Independence Rock on the horizon.
—Author photo

pleasure of some kind but we are selerabrating it by traviling in sand and dust," she muttered in her diary. But according to the next entry, Helen reached Independence Rock that evening and danced the night away.

In 1849 Margaret Judd wrote of a happy holiday encounter:

> On the fourth of July we camped for the day, not entirely to celebrate but to wash and do mending and various other things.... Well, we were making suds when a dapper young gentleman from New York, who was on his way to California, brought [me] a large piece of delicious fruit cake, which was made to celebrate the Fourth on the plains.... I accepted with great patriotism.

Frontier Pranksters

There was much "frontier humor" on the trail, and practical jokes became a ritual. In 1861 Zebulon Jacobs was a nineteen-year-old "down and back" driver, one of the young Mormon men who picked up emigrants in Nebraska and took them back to Utah. On the way to Nebraska, dozens of young men traveled together, and pranks were part of the package. Zeb told this story:

> About 10 o'clock we saw a man running towards us. We hailed him and found that he belonged to Heber C. Kimball's [down and back] train, which was a short distance ahead of us. The Utah Boys had induced him to catch rabbits in Yankee fashion by building a small fire and lying down by it with an open sack for the rabbits to run into, and then hit them on the head with a club, now and then giving a low whistle; other boys going out to drive the rabbits in. All of a sudden the boys gave a yell. The man thought the Indians were upon him, and off he started at full run. He had run about a mile when we stopped him.

Zebulon Jacobs (far left) with his brother, sister, and mother.
—Courtesy Brigham Young University

Camping near Scotts Bluff that year, Zeb and the same youths who had played the trick on the man awoke one morning to a surprise:

> *Everyone in the tent began laughing at each other's faces; come to find out we had all of our faces besmeared with tar and waggon grease. Some of the boys from the other camp paid us a visit and left their compliments upon our faces.*

Those young men must have been sound sleepers!

—SUMMARY—

Fun and recreation were important parts of the remarkable journey west. While pioneer children had none of the recreational and entertainment opportunities of today, they were more than willing to make their own fun. Later in life it was the happy occasions that were usually better remembered than the unpleasant ones. A sense of thanksgiving and hope is evident in the diaries and memoirs of those who followed their parents to the western frontier. Some journeys ended in health and prosperity, others in tragedy, but many shared the same happy trail experiences. Perhaps in reading about these experiences, modern young people can share the laughter, joy, and wonder of those who walked along that "longest road in the world" so many years ago.

Profile of
ELIZA ANN MCAULEY (EGBERT)

Eliza Ann McAuley (Egbert) with her husband, Robert Seely Egbert, on their wedding day. —*Courtesy Tom Macaulay*

Eliza Ann McAuley, born in Henry County, Iowa, on December 2, 1835, left a charming, dynamic diary. High-spirited, resolute, and dependable, Eliza was brave enough to wear bloomers in 1852 and saw nothing unfeminine about learning to shoot a pistol:

Monday, April 19th. This morning Tom [her brother] made me practice target shooting with his pistol. I was very expert at missing the mark, but managed to hit the tree three times out of five.

In 1852 Eliza's father, already in California, sent instructions to his wife to send the children ahead to join him. On the day of her departure, Eliza, age seventeen, mentions no sadness at leaving home and her mother:

Wednesday, April 7th, 1852. Bade adieu to home and started amid snow and rain for the land of gold. . . . We have a good sized tent and a sheet iron camp stove which can be set up inside, making it warm and comfortable, no matter what the weather outside. We have plentiful of provisions including dried fruits and vegetables, also a quantity of light bread cut in slices and dried for use when it is not convenient to bake. Our stove is furnished with a reflector oven which bakes very nicely. Our clothing is light and durable. My sister and I wear short dresses and bloomers and our foot gear includes a pair of light calf-skin topboots.

Eliza rode a horse during the journey west, and perhaps her bloomers (wide pants worn under a short dress, named for Amelia Bloomer, who urged women to wear them) permitted her to ride astride—a much safer way to ride than sidesaddle. Most women in those days considered it unladylike to wear bloomers and to ride astride.

Eliza recorded many details of her life on the trail in a five-by-seven-inch red notebook. When she ran out of ink on the journey, she made new ink with berries or plants she found along the way. Her journal is wonderful reading, exceptionally lively and imaginative. Ever optimistic and cheerful, Eliza seemed to enjoy herself very much on the journey, often observing with delight the sights and sounds of the trail:

> This afternoon we passed "Ancient Bluff Ruins" on the [north] side of the River, a picturesque mass of rocks, resembling castles and fortifications in ruins. Here a crumbling turret, there a bastion, and in other places portions of a wall, making the illusion complete.

Eliza and her siblings were in a well-organized company. The McAuleys were not poor and the children had plentiful provisions and sturdy equipment for the trip. There seems to have been no sickness in their camp, and Eliza and her siblings arrived in California in mid-September about as healthy as they were when they left Iowa—except, of course, they were a lot browner from the sun:

> Our first impression of Californians is that they are a very delicate people, as their complexions contrast so strongly with those of the sun-burned travelers on the plains.

California was good to Eliza Ann. In 1854 she married Robert Seely Egbert, and they eventually had seven healthy children. The couple found financial success and owned a large ranch in Solano County. After Robert's death in 1896, Eliza lived twenty-three more years.

Mr. Ezra Meeker, a traveling companion of the McAuleys famous for his work memorializing the Oregon Trail, had this to say about Eliza in his 1908 book *Ventures and Adventures of Ezra Meeker*:

> Eliza . . . a type of the healthy handsome American girl, graceful and modest, became the center of attraction upon which a romance might be written, but as the good elderly lady still lives the time has not yet come, and so we must draw the veil.

Eliza died in Berkeley in November 1919, a month before her eighty-fourth birthday.

Work, Study, and Discipline

I learned to turn with the lathe and ran the mill. I hunted wild turkeys, ducks, and squirrels and did some fishing. I learned from the Indians to paddle a canoe, fish with a spear, and shoot the bow and arrow.

—Autobiography of Thomas Cropper, age eleven in 1854

Both at home and on the trail, most children and teens in the 1800s had to pull their own weight. Day-to-day survival required serious labor, and families needed every member to pitch in. Parents expected to be obeyed and respected, and they reared their children with a strong work ethic. One rule was seldom violated: Chores must be finished before play can begin. It was part of their value system.

Child Labor

When family finances were tight, teens often sought employment outside the home. In the nineteenth century, there were no particular laws pertaining to hiring minors. Anyone willing and able to work for wages could do so. Just before his family's departure west in the spring of 1846, George Bean earned himself some money:

A little unpleasantness arose between me and Father, and I left home and went across the River April 1st, my fifteenth birthday, and got a job unloading a steamboat at Montrose, Iowa, [and] rec[eived] fifty cents per hour. . . . I carried four bushels of wheat at a load and would take a 'pig' of lead ore in each hand. . . . I made a few dollars and got more money than I ever had before . . . then returned home and took hold of duty as well as ever.

Fifty cents an hour was spectacular pay for a fifteen-year-old in 1846 (could George have meant per day?). Bushels of wheat weighed over fifty pounds each, and a "pig" of lead ore weighed about one hundred pounds. A few months later, George would use the money he saved to buy provisions for his sick family.

Coming from England in 1866, Ruth May did a brief stint in a cotton mill. This job was her introduction to the "Land of Opportunity":

My . . . sister and I, though not yet twelve years old . . . went to work. . . . I am sure it was no place for good girls. However we soon moved to Philadelphia. . . . My wage was a dollar a week and board. Thus we began to save and prepare for the journey to the [Salt Lake] Valley.

A dollar a week was a poor wage, but along with her board it was more than many children earned.

Earning a bit better pay was Heber McBride. Starting at age nine, Heber worked long hours in England to help his family of seven prepare for their migration:

I got a place as errand boy in a large Drug and Chimists store. I had to be on the go from 7 oclock in the morning till 9 oclock at night and Saterday nights till 10 oclock. . . . My wages was about half crown per week or about 60 cents American money, but that was very good wages for a small boy like me but I had to board and clothe myself. Father did not like to put me at very hard work [and] got me a place [taking tickets] in front of the Victoria Baths [public baths; he later became an attendant]. . . . [Soon] I was . . . getting 3 shillings per week [and later] was raised to 5 shillings per week, this was thought an outrageous price for a boy not quite 13 years old.

Five shillings was about $1.25 in American money.

The money young people earned was seldom spent on luxuries. Working to buy himself some shoes occupied some of twelve-year-old Jesse N. Smith's time in 1846: "During the summer I took a job of hoeing corn . . . thus earning the first pair of boots I ever owned."

Even children as young as seven earned their keep. Lucina Mecham gathered fruit in the present Council Bluffs, Iowa, area in 1847:

We picked wild grapes, strawberries, raspberries, gooseberries, black-berries, elderberries, also walnuts, hazelnuts, hickory nuts, and butternuts. Thus I earned my first pair of shoes. Up to this time my mother had made moccasins out of buckskins.

"Chipping In" on the Trail

If work was hard at home, it was doubly hard on the trail. Out of necessity, most young emigrants assumed major responsibilities. No one was exempt from helping out but the very young, the very old, the sick, and women who were about to give or had just given birth.

Youngsters' chores included herding cattle, milking cows, fetching water, caring for younger siblings, sewing, washing clothes, cooking, chopping wood, and hunting game. In addition to these familiar chores, which many young people had done regularly back home, there were a few new jobs on the trail, including gathering buffalo chips (dung). The pioneers used buffalo chips, also called prairie coal or meadow muffins, to fuel campfires on the plains, where wood was scarce. Chip gathering was an unsavory job, but the youngsters made it a little more fun with a chip song, which everyone knew:

> *Whoa, haw, Buck and Jerry Boy*
> *There's a pretty little girl in the outfit ahead*
> *Whoa, haw, Buck and Jerry Boy*
> *I wish she were by my side instead*
> *Whoa, haw, Buck and Jerry Boy*
> *Look at her now with a pout on her lips*
> *As daintily with her fingertips*
> *She picks for the fire some buffalo chips*
> *Whoa, haw, Buck and Jerry Boy.*

The names Buck and Jerry Boy referred to the oxen, which traveled so slowly that youngsters could pick up the chips as they moved along. As soon as the wagons stopped for the evening, parents sent the kids out with sacks to collect any dry chips they could find. If they were wise, they stockpiled some, too, or they would have to do without a fire when it rained. Because it wouldn't burn, a wet chip was a worthless chip, and besides, wet chips smelled!

Edwin Pettit described chip hunting as a thirteen-year-old in 1847:

> *Everyone would go out to gather buffalo chips and some of the daintier sex, instead of picking them up with their hands, used tongs but soon very bravely got over this and would almost fight over a dry one.*

During chip quests, the children often found surprises in the grass, as Rachel Emma Woolley, age twelve, discovered in 1848:

> *We would take a sack and fill it as we progressed. . . . [T]hey were very thick in a certain place close to the road, which was not often the case. . . . I thought I was in luck. I was picking up as fast as I could when I heard the rattle of a snake, [and] he was almost at my feet. I did not stop for any more chips at that time.*

Some amusing notes in the youngsters' journals tell of gathering buffalo chips. Seven-year-old Jesse Applegate, in the great Oregon company of 1843, was involved in a contest to see who could collect the most:

> Several of us boys were out . . . picking them up and throwing them into piles. . . . I remember a boy about my size with yellow sun-burnt hair and freckled face came over to our district and attempted to get away with a large chip, but I caught him in the act and threw another into his face with such violence as to . . . make the blood come. I think I was urged to this by the elder boys.

In spite of the occasional fights, such contests might have pleased the mothers. Chips were excellent fuel, but they burned fast and it took bushels of them to cook a meal. Most pioneers finally agreed: the only thing worse than buffalo chips was no buffalo chips. The French fur trappers had learned to burn *bois de vache* (cow's wood) in the eighteenth century. Indian women used buffalo chips combined with soft mosses for diapers. Who would have thought dung could be so useful?

Young Teamsters

Teamsters were those who drove the draft animals. If the teamster was driving horses or mules, he (or she) sat in the driver's seat of the wagon holding the reins and a whip. If oxen were pulling the wagon, the teamster walked along their left side with a prod. Team driving was enormously strenuous work, even for a grown man: the animals could be stubborn, the trail hazardous, and the labor exhausting. Teamsters guided the wagons across rocks, water, sand, and icy mountain passes. The four basic driving commands were "whoa" (stop), "giddup" (move), "haw" (go left), and "gee" (go right). These were words the animals understood (most of the time) and they are still in use today.

In 1848 John Smith, who turned sixteen on the trail, was in charge of several teams and helped get five wagons down Big Mountain, about twelve miles north of present Salt Lake City. Edward Henry Lenox was also a "lusty lad of 16" in 1843 when his family left for Oregon. His teamster skills made him the leader of the pack, but Edward gave the credit to his oxen:

> It was the virtues of this team that put me in the lead of our caravan all that summer. No matter how difficult the ford across a river, or how crooked it might be, [the oxen] responded readily to my every word and turned quickly to right or left at my least command. I drove . . . from Platte City, Missouri, to Whitman Station.

Crossing rivers was a special challenge. John Stoughton described a harrowing river crossing on his 1843 journey, when he was thirteen:

> [Famous missionary] Dr. Marcus Whitman saved my life in crossing [Idaho's] Snake River. We had chained about ten wagons together. . . . Dr. Whitman rode beside the wagon I had charge of, which was the hindmost wagon. . . . The current was very strong and came against the bank with terrible force [and] I got far behind. Dr. Whitman, seeing the danger I was in, wheeled around . . . and grabbed my horse by the bridle [and] we reached the island in safety.

Another young man of thirteen, Thales Haskall, was the only male traveling with his family when they trekked to Utah in 1847. He drove two yoke of oxen (four oxen total) for his mother. That same year, William Perry Nebeker, age eleven, also drove two yoke of oxen most of the way. Among those even younger was Albert Nephi Clements, who at nine became the chief teamster for his family on the way to Utah. "I drove the ox team most of the way across the plains," he remembered.

The youngest teamster must have been six-year-old Robert Sweeten, driving oxen on foot in 1847. Robert remembered this scene when he was ninety-two:

I walked most of the way across the plains, with but an occasional ride. One time I was driving two yoke of oxen so my stepfather could ride a while and rest. I stepped on a prickly pear, and being barefooted the needles ran into my feet. Mother had to pull them out.

Although driving teams was considered a male job, women and girls often stepped in when necessary. Mary Warner handled four horses at age fifteen. Matilda Ann Duncan was such a good teamster at age twelve that she drove the last five hundred miles to Utah in 1848 with no mishaps. This part of the trail was very hard to maneuver, so making it through without an accident was a rare accomplishment.

When a hired teamster left her family stranded in 1848, Rachel Emma Woolley's father handed her the reins of a frisky horse hitched to a buggy. She didn't have any choice but to drive:

My brother Frank was to drive a wagon, but he had to drive Mother. . . . so then I had to drive. I did so in fear and trembling, as one of the horses was very vicious. She used to kick up dreadful, but it made no difference. I had to go at it the next day just the same.

Sarah Norris, who had lost her father in the Battle of Nauvoo in September 1846, was in the driver's seat as the family pulled off a Mississippi ferry. "We made all haste to cross the river. We helped mother to her seat in the wagon . . . and I followed with the one horse wagon." Sarah's mother and her new baby died two months later. Now an orphan, Sarah showed her mettle by driving the entire journey to Utah at age thirteen.

Cowboys and Cowgirls

A chore related to teamstering was herding, which meant guiding the unyoked livestock along the trail, usually on horseback but sometimes on foot. Herders, like teamsters, were most often boys (cowboys), but there were a few working cowgirls. Fourteen-year-old Elizabeth Currier from Andrew County, Missouri, had that chore in 1846. Lizzy Flake, also fourteen, was a black slave who left for the Utah Valley in 1848 with her owner and drove the cattle the whole way. Etty Scott herded the livestock in 1852 at age eleven.

Herding was a hard and dirty job. According to trail lore, you had to "eat a peck of dust" before the journey ended. Sammy Burch remembered that dust seventy-five years later:

> I was in my seventeenth year when we crossed the plains. My job was to drive the loose cattle and if you want to know what dust is just drive a bunch of loose cattle on a windy day. You'll eat your peck of dust, all right.

A picturesque account by author Thomas L. Kane described some daring boys in the summer of 1846 getting oxen across the Missouri River at Council Bluffs:

> I have seen the youths, in stepping from back to back of the struggling monsters, or swimming in among their battling hoofs, display feats of . . . hardihood, that would have made . . . a Madrid bull-ring vibrate with bravos of applause.

It would be a mistake to presume that every young pioneer performed his chores with the utmost reliability and good cheer. Of course there was a hint of resistance at times. This 1853 account from Mrs. Amelia Stewart Knight describes her husband trying to get their teenage sons to get ready in the morning. While few modern boys would have these particular chores, in spirit these parent-child exchanges are the same as they are today.

> Monday, June 27th. "Children, all hands help yoke these cattle." . . . Plutarch [age sixteen] answers: "I can't. I must hold the tent up, it is blowing away." "Hurry boys, Who tied these horses? Seneca, don't stand there with your hands in your pocket. Get your saddles and be ready."

Guard Duty

When a wagon train camped for the night, the young men in the company, rifles in hand, took turns standing guard over the cattle to keep them from being stolen or just wandering off. It was extremely hard to walk and work all day, then have to stand watch at night. Some boys pulled a handcart all day, with no food, and still had to do guard duty. Emigrant Agnes Caldwell remembered a watch in 1856, when she was nine:

> One very cold night, some young men were on guard. Mother prepared some meat broth, and gave each one of the young men a half pint. They often declared it saved their lives and never before or since had anything tasted so good.

The motto in camp was "Eternal vigilance is the price for safety." Most companies assigned guard duty in four-hour shifts, sometimes longer. Henry P. Richards, age seventeen, was in charge of two teams when he traveled to Utah in 1848, and he stood watch "half the night every third night for the entire time."

Elisha Brooks was teamster and guard at age eleven. Years later he described going after some cattle that Indians had stolen in the night:

> One of my brothers and I were standing our watch one night. I remember how clear and bright the midnight stars looked. Suddenly an Indian yell rent the air [and] our skeleton beasts sprang up and away like a whirlwind. We dared not follow in the dark for fear of ambuscades, but, at the first streak of dawn, we were riding hard, ten men and a boy armed for trouble. . . . It was sundown the next day before we got back to camp. The cattle, too weak to travel very far, were found.

John Steele, eighteen, was on guard duty when a potentially deadly tornado hit his camp:

May 23. Soon after midnight a dark, portentous mass came mov-
ing down. . . . The oxen [became] uneasy. . . . Suddenly, with a
tremendous swoop, it burst upon us; nearly every tent was swept
from its fastening, and the flood of rain which followed drenched
the unfortunates whose bed clothes whirled in the wind . . . [so]
we found it necessary to hold on by the grass to prevent being blown
from our place at the opening of the corral.

Usually the guards were boys over fourteen, but when the need arose, younger boys met the challenge—twins Elisha and Elijah Brooks were just eleven. There was at least one eight-year-old guard in an 1847 Mormon group camped at the forks of the Platte River. But the boy, perhaps *too* young, caused a major stampede. George Bean wrote in his journal:

Washington Cook and a boy, Amenzo Baker [were] on guard sit-
ting at the opening. Some of the cattle moved to go out and the boy,
having a sheep-skin over his shoulders, shook the skin to scare the
animals back. It rattled [and] in an instant, with one snort, the
whole herd was on the full run through the lines. . . . 46 head were
lost. . . . This circumstance caused a week's delay.

Occasionally girls assisted in guarding the herds, too. In 1864 fifteen-year-old Mary Eliza Warner helped keep watch at night so the men could get some rest. Though she wasn't armed, she was ready to sound a warning should trouble come.

Many mysterious events occurred during guard duty. Charley True remembered a nightmare incident in 1859, when he was sixteen:

I had eaten my last hard-tack [a dry biscuit] and taken a linger-
ing look at the wonders of that solemn night . . . eager to turn in
between the blankets. . . . We had heard no disturbance whatever.
Then [we discovered] every hoof was gone. . . . They had gone from
us in the darkness . . . swallowed up by the earth.

Charley must have been exhausted the day after his herd disappeared, for he got no sleep that night, searching for his lost cattle.

Stalking Dinner

On the trail, hunting was an essential means of getting food, and the job fell principally to young men and boys. By the time a boy was sixteen, he knew how to shoot and often had his own rifle. One newspaper article of the day captured a typical scene as the wagons rolled westward:

> *Keen-eyed youngsters, with their chins yet smooth and their rifles on their shoulders kept in advance of the wagons with long strides, looking as if they were already watching around the corners for game.*

Hunting skill helped Stephen I. Bunnell put meat on the table at age fourteen:

> *My father moved to ... Iowa and lived there with five other families. We came very near starving to death the winter of 1848. Our provisions was all gone about Feb the 20. I at that time was detained as hunter for the camp on account of my excellent good luck with the gun.*

Naturally, hunting was dangerous. In addition to gunshot accidents, hunters risked getting lost or encountering threatening wild animals. Seventeen-year-old emigrant Moses Shallenberger had a nerve-racking experience near Independence Rock in 1844. Out hunting buffalo, he and a friend had an uneasy encounter. The young men must have been expert hunters, for they had killed two buffaloes. As they cut the meat up for easier hauling, some hungry wolves appeared, growling and snarling. The boys were forced to keep guard all night. At dawn, as the wolves were still sniffing around, an even more ferocious animal appeared and drove them off. A bear had smelled the blood. Moses recalled:

As soon as it became light enough to shoot, [we] attempted to kill the bear, but he went away. We finished butchering the game, but left some pieces for the wolves.

In her diary of her trip west in 1864, Mrs. James Rousseau mentions one young man with a superior ability to bring home the bacon. He was the sixteen-year-old son of Nicholas Earp, the captain of the wagon train. The boy's name was Wyatt, "who with his rifle kept his family in meat to California." In about twenty years, Wyatt Earp would become a legend as a lawman of the Wild West.

Mother's Helpers

Most girls didn't need to learn cooking, sewing, nursing, and babysitting skills on the trail because they were already experts. In those days girls helped with homemaking chores as soon as they were able. Some chores, such as cooking, were a bit trickier to perform under trail conditions, however. When her family emigrated west in 1856, twelve-year-old Mary Powell was the family cook:

Each day I took pains to watch the women bake bread in their bake-kettles. I knew that I should have to do the baking when our own kettle came and I was anxious to learn. . . . I took the kettle and went off . . . took dough and made twenty four beautiful brown biscuits. I was glad as glad could be. I took the biscuits to camp and surprised Mother.

In addition to her hard work as a cook, Mary proved to be a marvel on the trail in other ways:

Mother was getting faint with thirst. . . . I walked more than ten miles extra to get Mother a drink. I ran part of the way [and] secured water for her.

Often a daughter's chores increased with the arrival of a new member of the family. Emigrant father James Smithies made several approving comments about his ten-year-old daughter, Mary, after his wife gave birth on July 5, 1847: "My little dau[ghter] Marey has washed all our clothes today." Later he added, "My little daughter Marey and myself we do our own cooking & washing so that we do not have to trouble any one."

Mary Field said she did just about *everything* as a sixteen-year-old on her family's overland trek:

> After starting west again I helped to tend and yoke the oxen and took my turn driving them as I had to walk most of the way across the plains because there was not enough room in the wagon for all of us. I would help Mother tend the children and prepare our meals.

Just as young women and girls often did "men's work," men and boys performed domestic chores at times. At seventeen, John McWilliams was in an all-male company in 1849 and helped cook, a new experience for him:

> After we arrived [at St. Joseph] and went into camp, father found us cooking supper. I was cutting meat, another boy was making bread, and another was making coffee.

On the trail, one never knew what might happen, and when problems arose children often had to take on even more responsibility. The Thomas McNeil family came to America from Scotland in 1856 to join a Mormon handcart company. En route to Genoa, Nebraska, two years later, the family was delayed because of runaway cattle. Eleven-year-old Margaret became a surrogate mother:

> The company had gone ahead, and my mother was anxious to have me go, so she strapped my little brother James on my back with a shawl. He was only four years old and still quite sick with the measles ... so I hurried on and caught up with the company. I traveled with them all day ... [and then] I sat up and held

*James in my lap with a shawl wrapped around him, alone all
night. We traveled this way for a week, my brother and I not seeing our mother during this time.*

School on the Go

American public education during the nineteenth century was
variable at best, and the emphasis put on academics differed from
family to family. On the trail, with no schools or teachers and few
books, education was apt to be overlooked altogether. Ann Cannon, age fourteen in 1847, had books en route to Utah, but she put
other things before lessons:

> *When I did not have to drive, I rode with George Q. [her brother].
> He said: "Now, Annie, get your books and I will teach you." "Oh, I
> have not time; it takes me all the time I get to fix my clothes." I
> missed the best opportunity I ever had. I have been very sorry I
> missed it.*

Some families, however, insisted that their children study.
William M. Colvig's mother did not allow him any excuses:

> *Mother had reduced the library to just a few books—the Bible, a
> hymn book, Pilgrim's Progress, Frost's Pictorial History of the United
> States, Webster's Elementary Spelling Book, and Mcguffey's First
> and Second Readers. During the six months or more we were on
> the plains, Mother had me recite to her, so that by the end of the
> trip I was reading in the Second Reader.*

It is no surprise that William, who was six in 1851, later became
a lawyer, then a judge in Oregon.

Often children had to wait until they reached their destination
before they had the opportunity to study seriously. Even after families settled into their new homes, there may or may not have been
a school nearby. Many youngsters were self-taught. As a young gold

miner, John McWilliams, who took off for California in 1849 at age seventeen, spent his nights in scholarly pursuits. John had to send away for his books:

I sent in to Mr. Weber, the trader at Shasta [California], and asked if he could not send me a book to read. He sent me Plutarch's Lives leather-bound, and said if I liked it I should send him five dollars. Well, I turned it over, and there were the names of Solon, Theseus, Romulus, Lycurgus and other names of which I knew nothing.... I read about Timoleon. From that I got to reading the whole book.

Strict Discipline

"Spare the rod and spoil the child" was a motto that many nineteenth-century parents took to heart. The kinds of physical punishment children received then would be considered child abuse by today's standards, but disciplinary methods such as whipping children with a rope or small tree limb, called a switch, were common in those days.

If children disobeyed their parents or did not do their chores, punishment was usually swift and sometimes severe. Yet most youngsters expected the consequences and saw punishment as a parent's duty. Rachel Emma Woolley recalled her whippings without resentment:

At night when we camped we would rush for the river to bathe. [Once] I was disobedient and went with the girls as usual. We staid longer than usual and the night being very dark I lost my way.... I found Father with a rope in his hand waiting to receive me. I got a deserved warm reception.

Did the punishment always fit the crime? No. Sometimes adults were fanatical about being obeyed, and punishment was a means of control. Although Rachel didn't seem to object to her parents' disciplinary measures, Matilda Jane Sager remembered her childhood in a foster home as horrific. "For several years I was never without welts or black and blue marks," Matilda recalled. She continued:

Children didn't ask questions in those days. They obeyed orders. . . . From the time I was eight [in 1847], until I was 15 I was whipped so much that I got to feeling about it as one does the winter rain — that it was inevitable and was to be borne without complaint. . . . Childhood was a time of terror and bitterness when I was a girl.

Fortunately, abuse this extreme was rare.

Heavier Burdens

Most pioneer children had serious responsibilities, but hardship forced some into full-fledged adult roles. David C. Hess was ten when his father died in June 1846. His older brother John left to join the Mormon Battalion. David became the man of the house and helped provide for three younger siblings. He helped build a cottage made of bark elm and "put in a small farm of buckwheat and corn for the support of the family." After his brother returned in 1849, the family was ready to head for Utah. David credited "Providence" with giving them the means to go west:

A couple of gold seekers en route to California met [my] brother John, and for the sum of $250.00 employed him as their guide to the Rocky Mountains. About May 2, 1849 we began our long perilous journey across the Plains. Our outfit consisted of two yoke of oxen, one yoke of cows, a pioneer wagon and twenty head of sheep. Barefoot and half clad though I was, the burden of driving the sheep fell upon me, then in my twelfth year.

Two of the most heroic young people in the Mormon exodus, Ellen and Aurelia Spencer, fourteen and twelve, also had serious responsibilities in 1846. As Aurelia remembered it:

Ellen had to see after the other children and the tent work, as we were living in a tent. So it fell to my lot to be nurse, as I went along to take care of George [a younger brother], and was with ma when she died. . . .

We kept house by ourselves. . . . It was well for us that we had been taught to knit and sew, for we had our own clothes to mend and look after. . . . We got through the first part of the winter pretty well, as father had provided for our wants, having left us with eight cows and one horse; [but] the horse was sold for provisions.

These two girls looked after their four other siblings for two years while their father was away, and again later in Utah. Despite the hard work, the children found time to play games, tell stories, and have spelling and reading lessons. Aurelia earned a few cents during that time by taking in sewing and making jewelry out of hair.

Because of their poverty, the Mormons who pushed handcarts, having neither covered wagons nor draft animals, probably worked the hardest of any emigrants and suffered the most from exposure and hunger. Sarah James, age seventeen in 1856, and other teenagers pulled carts all the way to Fort Bridger in southwestern Wyoming before getting to ride in a wagon.

Peter McBride, brother of Heber, had a vivid memory of being in a handcart company in 1856, when he was just six, concerning his sixteen-year-old sister:

My mother was sick all the way over, and my sister Jeanetta had the worry of us [five] children. She carried water from the river to do the cooking. Her shoes gave out, and she walked through the snow barefoot, actually leaving bloody tracks in the snow.

Many pioneer children became orphans, and the older siblings had to carry the load. Ann Cannon took on adult duties the first year at Winter Quarters, and later in Utah:

We washed on the bank of a creek. . . . Sometimes I would tread the clothes in the bed of the stream with my bare feet. . . . Aunt Leonora [Taylor] was sick with rheumatism and there was a big family to do for. . . . We had a grist mill but the water to run it was frozen. . . . The Lord only knows how we got along.

—SUMMARY—

On the frontier, children had responsibilities many young people today could scarcely imagine. Youngsters helped with daily tasks, drove cattle, even supported their families. But the young pioneers seldom saw themselves as victimized or overworked, and there is little record of children complaining or displaying disrespect on the trail. On the contrary, the young emigrants performed their duties with amazing maturity and showed courage in times of adversity.

Profile of
LIZZY FLAKE (ROWAN)

Lizzy Flake (Rowan). —Courtesy
San Bernardino County Museum

Lizzy Flake's life reads like a heroic saga. Another young pioneer who zig-zagged across much of the United States during the great exodus west between 1843 and 1867, she was different in one way: she was a slave. After walking across the plains with her owners, who were fleeing Nauvoo, Lizzy ended up in California with her freedom and moderate wealth. Like many young pioneers, she made her life a success.

Lizzy was born in 1833 in Anson County, North Carolina, on the plantation of William Love. Her relatives picked cotton and did much of the other work on the Love estate. In 1838 Lizzy became the personal slave of William Love's daughter Agnes, who had just married James M. Flake. As was customary for slaves, Lizzy took the last name of her owners. Agnes and James soon moved to Mississippi and joined the Mormon Church. In 1844 they moved to Nauvoo, Illinois. They had three young sons by then, and Lizzy, just eleven, took care of the boys. One son died in Nauvoo.

The Mormons fled Nauvoo in early 1846 and began their journey toward the Rocky Mountains. They didn't get very far that first year. During the winter of 1846–47, the family lived in a dugout, and later a cabin, in Winter Quarters, Nebraska, where the Mormons made a temporary settlement before continuing west. Between 1846 and 1848, two other children were born to the Flakes, but only one, a daughter named Sarah James, survived.

By 1848 the Flakes were ready for the long journey to the Valley of the Great Salt Lake, where some Mormons had settled the previous year. On the trail, Lizzy not only tended to the two boys and helped with new baby Sarah James, she also performed domestic chores and herded cattle. Fortunately, the boys were old enough to help. About twenty other black children walked the trail with the Mormons in 1848.

Utah was not to be the permanent residence of the Flake family. Two years after they arrived, James Flake decided to join a group of Mormons moving on to California to start a settlement there. By now Lizzy was seventeen, so she had major responsibilities during the journey. Among other things, she was in charge of the ox team. In two years, Lizzy walked over 2,300 miles.

In June 1850, soon after their arrival in California, James Flake died. The next year, Lizzy helped his two sons, William and Charles, construct the first adobe house built by Mormons in the San Bernardino Valley. Tragedy hit the Flake family again about 1853, when Agnes became very ill, leaving Lizzy in charge of the household and the children. William, sixteen by then, took his father's place as head of the family.

One night Agnes grew weaker, and she called Lizzy to awaken the children. While Agnes was giving her children her final counsel on how to live good lives, Lizzy went to get two neighbor women. When she returned, Agnes was dead. As Liz wept, one of the women made a negative comment about Agnes. Liz took the woman by the shoulders and screamed:

You can't talk like that about my mistress when she isn't able to defend herself. She was the best woman that lived; she was not mean to me, she never hit me; I love her better than anyone in the world. You can't stay in this house.

Lizzy never spoke to that woman again.

Lizzy grieved deeply; Agnes had been like a mother to her. Now Lizzy became mother to the Flake children. She kept house and took care of them until the fall of 1855, when they returned to Utah. Before they left, Lizzy told William, "Marry and I will come and serve you and your family the rest of my life." But California was a free state, and William told her she should stay there and have a family of her own. She said she didn't want her freedom, but he asked her to stay and think about it. Lizzy went to live with an older black woman who had crossed the plains with the Flake family.

Twenty-two at the time, Lizzy was soon dating some of the black men in the area. The suitor who won her hand, Charles H. Rowan, owned and operated a barber shop nearby. He had been a teamster with a Utah company before traveling on to San Bernardino. The newlyweds bought a corner lot with a building on it in a desirable business area. The first floor became Charles's barber shop; they set up housekeeping upstairs.

Eventually they had three children—a daughter named Alice and two sons. Lizzy made sure her children were well educated, and Alice became a schoolteacher of white children in about 1875, a rare distinction according to historic records: "It has been said that this was the first time in the United States where a colored girl taught in a white school." A son, Byron Rowan, owned and operated a successful garage north of town. He had friends of both races and was well liked by everyone.

Lizzy did not forget her first family. She kept in touch with William Flake, who moved to Arizona and got married in 1858. By then the Rowans had acquired a little wealth. Lizzy showed her devotion to William in choosing a valuable set of silverware for his wedding gift, some of which is still owned and treasured by William's descendants.

Lizzy became well known in the San Bernardino area and was considered a wonderful mother and wife and a great pioneer in her own right. She died in 1903 at the age of seventy. Her impressive granite marker can still be seen in the cemetery in San Bernardino.

Encounters with Native Americans

It was with magnificent terror that [I] kept on going to-wards these Indians whose faces remained immobile and solemn. . . . I gave one wild yell, and made a wild dash to get by, whereupon there was a peal of laughter from the three Indians. They say Indians never laugh, but I learned differently.

—Autobiography of Harry (B. H.) Roberts, age nine in 1866

There were many comments in the journals of westering Americans revealing the typical fear of and misconceptions about Indians. Young people heading out on the trail heard horror stories of kidnappings, killings, and scalpings—some true, some not. But when the young emigrants actually met the natives, they found that most were not hostile, and their fear often turned to fascination.

Not only were most natives friendly to the pioneers, but in fact the success of America's western expansion was due in part, rather ironically, to Indian help. One of the most historically significant instances of Indian guidance occurred in the 1844 party to which eighteen-year-old Moses Shallenberger belonged. They were be-friended by a Paiute man, whose name they wrote as Truckee. He told them of a river they could follow through the Sierra Nevada. The grateful emigrants named the river after him.

Early Oregon-bound travelers depended on native guides to get them down the Columbia by canoe or raft. This was the only way to get to the Oregon coast before the Barlow Road opened. Indians also helped ferry many emigrants across other rivers on the trail. Some girls in a 1857 handcart company received a much-needed ride across the Loup Fork of the Platte River, though it may have been socially uncomfortable for these strictly raised, modest young ladies, according to the captain of the company, famous artist C. C. A. Christensen:

> A large Indian encampment was located at that time right at the fording place, and several of the young girls were ferried across by sitting behind a half-naked Indian on horseback, having to hold on to him around the waist in order not to fall off.

During the cold, lean winter of 1846–47, two tribes, the Omaha and the Pottowatamie, did much to help the nearly starving Mormon families wintering at Council Bluffs, Iowa, and Winter Quarters, Nebraska, after they were driven from Nauvoo. The Indians let the emigrants camp on their land and gave them supplies on credit or in exchange for cattle and what little grain the Saints could spare. The Mormons also helped protect the Indians from their enemies and taught some of the native children to read.

In spite of the mostly friendly exchanges between whites and Indians, the pioneers remained wary. Frequent rumors of imminent Indian attacks frazzled nerves on the trail. Seventeen-year-old Helen Stewart wrote of one man, John, in her 1853 company who was particularly jumpy:

> Today we heard great word of the indians, they say there is five hundred of them going to fight. . . . But the great army that frightened [us] proved to be very friendly. . . . I do not know wether old John has got over his panic yet or not.

First Impressions

The words "Beware of Indians" were probably still ringing in Edwin Pettit's ears when he met his first ones in 1847. Edwin, just thirteen, was assigned to search for a lost calf:

> [One] morning I was sent back several miles to bring in [the] calf. . . . I saw four Indians coming. I was riding a good horse, and had a good half mile start. They came up, talked to me and [then] they let me pass. It is almost a miracle they did not take my horse as it was a very good one. I found the calf and returned to my company. . . . We saw many Indians, but for the most part they were very friendly.

Eleven-year-old Elisha Brooks's first encounter with Indians sent him into panic in 1852:

> As we drew near Council Bluffs on the Missouri River, the cry of "Indians, Indians," turned me to stone. Just ahead, a band of blanketed, feathered, beaded, fringed, wild looking objects barred our way. I thought our days were numbered. I slunk under the wagon in abject terror, peering through the wheels to watch the proceedings.

As it turned out, the Indians were merely looking to trade for some food.

While the emigrants were afraid of the Indians, the Indians were also wary of the emigrants. Edward Lenox, age sixteen in 1843, later recorded how one tribe reacted to his wagon party's approach:

> All of a sudden we came into view. There was a quick yell to their horse guards. . . . Men and squaws and children altogether tore down the wigwams. They ran to their ponies, the squaws lashed the tent-poles to them, leaving the ends dragging on the ground. Tepees, buffalo robes, cooking utensils, provisions, and everything

pertaining to the village was gathered up in an incredible short space of time.... They were afraid of our "walking lodges."

Elisha Brooks, who had crawled underneath his wagon in "abject terror" at his first Indian sighting, later learned to travel with a Crow tribe in complete harmony:

On the Sweetwater River, we came across a band of friendly Crow Indians moving camp in search of better hunting grounds. They traveled with us a week or more marching by day in our front and on our flanks and erecting their wigwams near us at night.... We were a wild west show.

Culture Shock

Indian culture and customs could be mystifying to outsiders like the pioneers. Emigrant diaries often conveyed a sense of wonder when describing Indians and their ways. Some comments reveal the pioneers' prejudices and misconceptions, and they found some Indian practices of the day outright shocking. Certainly there were profound differences between native society and their own, and they generally did not hold back when expressing their opinions about it.

Granville Stuart, on the California Trail at seventeen in 1852, later moved to Montana and lived among the local Indians. He left detailed observations of one village he visited:

Some of the lodges were painted and decorated with colored drawings; these drawings represented victorious battles or horse-stealing. When an Indian possessed one of these decorated lodges he would not sell it.... The women do all the work even to saddling and unsaddling the horses for their lords and masters. Girls are taught to do all the work which falls to the mother's lot, when they are very young.

One Indian practice that surprised the emigrants was the way they utilized dogs. They trained some of the large dogs to carry huge loads. Seventeen-year-old Welborn Beeson observed this scene near Fort Laramie on June 6, 1853:

We passed a [Sioux] Indian village. They have their dogs trained to haul two poles fastened to each side and one end dragging on the ground with a keg fastened across the poles just behind the dog, they then hauled their water and their children about. They haul their wigwams about in the same manner, only they have horses for that.

The five Hays sisters of Illinois were heading to California in 1853 when they saw a band of Indians going by. The eldest sister, Miss Lorena Hays, penned in her diary:

One poor dog seemed to have too heavy a load and laid down howling most piteously—no one seemed to notice him while passing, and at last he got up and followed on again.

Another custom that particularly fascinated the young pioneers was how the Plains Indians interred their dead up in trees or on scaffolding. The Indians believed it put the deceased souls closer to heaven. One camp clerk, Mr. William Clayton, vividly described the entombment of an infant near Grand Island, Nebraska, in 1847:

In one of the large ash trees in the middle of the camp is an Indian babe or papoose. It cannot be said to be buried, but deposited . . . being first wrapped with a skin and then tied between two of the higher limbs of the tree. The bark is all peeled off from below to prevent wolves from getting up.

Young Mary Anderson and her brother were among those who found a typical treetop grave, and Mary left an account:

Scaffolding upon which Plains Indians placed their dead. —Courtesy LDS
Historical Department Archives

*My twin brother, N. O. Anderson, and I were just nine years old
when we crossed the plains. We would run alongside the wagons
while traveling, and of course, we kept our eyes open all the way
for signs of danger. One day we came by a tree that had a scaffold
of some kind in it. We decided to find out what it was. We climbed
up all right, but came down a lot faster. He saw a dead Indian
with butcher knives and a gun by his side. That was the last time
we ever snooped into anything like that.*

Because intertribal battles were commonplace among most
tribes, pioneers sometimes witnessed Indian war rituals. The victory celebration was one they viewed with some repugnance. Mr.
George Read watched this event in 1850 near Council Bluffs:

*We saw here a large collection of the Pottawatamie warriors, as-
sembled to have a war dance over two scalps of their enemies the*

Pawnees, a tribe which is situated on the Platte. They cook and eat the feet, hands and heart of their slain.

Mr. Frederick A. Cooper, member of a handcart company, had an unusual invitation in the Devil's Gate area in 1859:

The victorious tribe was parading around with scalps suspended on sticks which they held high in the air. They had a number of prisoners. They invited a number of us boys to go to their camp that night to witness them [execute] their prisoners. However, we respectfully declined.

Perhaps even more shocking to the pioneers than war rituals was the Indian practice of selling women and children. Though at the time some whites were still trading black slaves in the southern United States, many emigrants were opposed to that as well. Ann Ward, a nine-year-old emigrant from England, arrived at Council Bluffs in 1857, where she encountered some natives apparently desperate for food:

Large numbers of Indians came around the boat begging [and] tried to get bread and money. One of them had an infant about two weeks, a male child and white as if it had been born of white parents. She offered to sell the child for 75 cents.

Other accounts also mentioned Indians wanting to trade children for goods. Several Mormons, who were abolitionists, bought Indian children to keep them from being sold into slavery.

An Indian habit the emigrants found especially irksome was cattle and horse stealing. Capturing animals was a way for young Indian men to prove their prowess and enhance their reputation. It was a rare company that did not experience at least one Indian attempt to take some of their livestock, and these episodes often resulted in brief conflicts.

Successful cattle and horse raids could be devastating to the targeted parties. Indians stole all the animals in the company of Barsina Rogers, age thirteen, and her family as they were camped in New Mexico en route to Arizona in 1867. Her sister remembered the episode:

> The indians crept up during the dark and jumped up suddenly, the horses broke the stake ropes and the Indians ran them up a canyon [and] got all of them but one, a fine Stallion. They left him full of poison arrows.

Judging by Appearances

Indian dress also fascinated and sometimes perplexed the outsiders. Some tribes wore far less covering than members of polite Victorian society were used to. Other times pioneers were awestruck at the sight of elaborate ceremonial costumes. Charley True, sixteen at the time, recalled that he was eating a typical trail lunch of hardtack and milk in 1859 when he encountered a party of Sioux in battle garb. Little wonder he remembered this scene:

> Suddenly, without warning, there stood at the edge of our circle near a bunch of willows, a splendid athletic specimen of an Indian, wearing a jaunty beaded buckskin suit. . . . The last to drop in upon us seemed quite a young man. Fringed leggings of antelope skin encased his limbs, leaving his lithe figure bare to the waistline. His moccasins were profusely decorated with the porcupine quills. Above his broad forehead there was an elaborate plume of bright colored feathers—the badge of a chief. Small ear pendants of shells were attached to each earring. His bearing was noble, impressive and wildly picturesque.

Mr. J. Goldsborough Bruff recorded his impressions of a typical young Indian woman, probably Shoshone, whom he saw at Fort Hall in 1849:

A young Indian ... came up, and leaned against the railing opposite the door. . . . She was about 18 yrs of age, rather tall, and slender, of a very light yellow complexion, glossy black hair, done up in long braids, with ribbons, like our school-girls, black eyes & long lashed: Her dress was pure white deer-skin, reaching a little below the knees; pantaloons to the ankle, moccasins, and a purple Merino shawl, thrown gracefully around her waist, and over one arm.

Some emigrants saw Indians getting ready for war or returning from a victory and were terrified. In 1846 Lucy Henderson, eleven, and her fourteen-year-old friend Elizabeth Currier stopped at Fort Laramie, where they were frightened yet intrigued at the sight of a native battle ritual. Lucy recalled:

While we were stopping at Fort Laramie, the Indians gave a war dance and I was scared nearly to death. They were nearly naked, and all painted, and they jumped and yelled and brandished their tomahawks while the fire around which they danced lit up their savage faces. There was one young squaw who was really pretty. She had on a shirt of beautifully beaded and nicely tanned buckskin, but I was afraid of Indians so I didn't go very close to her.

While many times the pioneers found the natives' appearance intimidating, in other cases Indian attire might even seem humorous to them. Eighteen-year-old Elmeda S. Harmon, camped with the Mormons in Nebraska in 1848, remembered a small boy wearing a ribbon in an unusual place:

The Indians were dressed, what little clothing they wore, in buckskin. . . . I noticed a little black-eyed Indian boy about three years old entirely naked except a bright red ribbon tied around his peepee.

A Ute boy.
—Courtesy LDS
Historical
Department
Archives

A Matter of Taste

Indians lived off the land. They utilized whatever nature provided them to survive. The Plains tribes hunted buffalo, which was their main food staple. They dried the meat and used it all winter. It was a common saying on the trail that the Indians used all parts of the buffalo "except the voice." They made clothing, blankets, and tents from the hide; fashioned jewelry from the teeth, hooves, and horns; and ate just about everything else. In addition to buffalo meat, some tribes ate salmon and other fish as well as game animals including deer, rabbit, and even wolf. Many Indians ate corn and wild plant foods such as sego lilies, thistles, seeds, acorns, and nuts.

Some foods the natives ate seemed peculiar to the pioneers. For example, many western tribes, especially the Shoshone and Ute, ate crickets and grasshoppers. Benjamin Bonney, only eight at the time, was offered a strange concoction in 1846 and gave it a try:

We came to an Indian camp. The Indians were living on dried acorns and crickets. The crickets were very large. The way the Indians prepared them was to catch the crickets, pull off their hind legs so they couldn't hop away, pile them in the sun and let them dry, then mix them with the acorns, put them all together in a stone mortar and make a sort of bread out of them. The squaws gave us children some of this black bread, which looked like fruit cake, but had a different taste. Some of us ate, but others were rather squeamish and didn't care to taste it.

Seventeen-year-old John McWilliams was aghast at the dish he saw one Indian woman prepare in 1849:

A squaw was making dinner and took a pup—a young one—and strangled it right before me. Then she threw it on the fire and singed it, scraped it, and cut it up. Then she put it in the pot to cook. . . . I did not stop for dinner.

Bows and Arrows

Not many tribes used guns when the great western migration first began. Most Native Americans were experts, however, with bows and arrows. Mr. Frederick Piercy wrote of this rivalry between two young Indian men:

Friday, June 17, 1853. I asked one of the young men to give me a specimen of his skill in shooting with the bow. He fixed a small cracker on a stick which he stuck in the ground, and standing about 12 yards from it, aimed 2 or 3 times but did not hit it. A still younger one, seeing his want of skill, impatiently took his place, and split the cracker with the first arrow.

Welborn Beeson also witnessed some natives with superior archery skills in 1853:

There are a great many little squirrels similar to the Illinois ground squirrel which the Indians shoot with arrows. They can hit one every time through the head. They stand and watch their holes and when the little fellow sticks out his [head] he is a goner. Two Indians just passed the tent with a great load of them.

The Indians occasionally used their bow-and-arrow skills against the emigrants' horses and livestock. Mormon company leader Henry William Bigler describes a remarkable episode in 1847:

We were followed all day by Indians. . . . Late in the evening we found that one of our horses was shot with a poison arrow. . . . We showed the wounded horse [to the Indians] and took their arrows. They pow-wowed over the animal when the one Indian put his mouth over the wound and sucked out all the poison and the wound healed up and the next morning we gave them their bows . . . and let them go.

Let's Make a Deal

One of the favorite activities in most camps was trading with the Indians. Young pioneers bartered for moccasins, ponies, buffalo skins, edible roots, salmon, and meat in exchange for tobacco, nails, trinkets, guns, shirts, shoes, flour, sugar, and coffee. Many emigrants going to Oregon owed their lives to trading with Indians for salmon and other food along the Columbia River.

Elisha Brooks, age eleven, helped his mother trade for moccasins in 1852. The exchange was seven safety pins for one pair of moccasins. One woman discovered she had received eight pins and dangled her prize in front of the other women. They all came back demanding another pin, which they got. Another special trade kept Elisha busy afterward:

Our mother bought a fine pony for a blanket and a pint of sugar, and I mounted him bare backed with a hackamore bridle, in Indian fashion to try him out. I never had been on a horse before, and he, discovering that it certainly was no Indian astride of him ran away with me . . . and found me wanting to get off and walk.

Seventeen-year-old Eliza Ann McAuley, one of the few young women to mingle and trade with Indians, found much to admire in the Shoshone. The McAuleys camped for about a week near Soda Springs in 1852 to rest and let their cattle feed. On July 21, "a very intelligent Indian named Poro" visited their camp with his small son, and Eliza ordered some moccasins, delivered several days later:

July 27. Poro brought our moccasins. They are very neatly made. His little boy came with him. I offered a gay plaid shawl in payment for the moccasins. Poro was quite pleased with it and inclined to accept it, but refered the matter to the boy. He talked to his father, who explained [to us] that he thought it was very pretty but he could not eat it. He wanted bread and sugar, so we gave him what he wanted.

Trading with the natives gave emigrants the perfect opportunity to learn more about their customs, values, and language, and vice versa. When Poro came to Eliza's camp, "He interpreted [some] Indian words for us. . . . It pleased him very much to see us try to learn it," Eliza wrote. "He seems to understand the customs of the whites very well," she added. Although Eliza had been afraid of the first Indians she met, by the time she was midway to California she was trading, socializing, and learning some of their language.

Welborn Beeson bargained with the Sioux in 1853, to their mutual delight. Of interest in Welborn's trade is that many emigrants said the Indians would not accept money, but obviously these Sioux did:

> *I bought a buffalo skin of an Indian, Paid him $4.00 for it. I put it over my shoulders the same as they wear them. There were several squaws about and they seemed very much pleased to see me dressed their fashion.*

As we learned earlier, Indians did not limit their trading to objects and animals. Natives often made offers to buy wives from among the whites. Redheaded and blond women were of special interest, and the family lore of many pioneer descendants includes a story claiming that they received a spectacular offer from some wealthy chief for their fair-haired daughter or sister. Mr. Andrew Chambers wrote of the deal some natives in the Umatilla Valley wanted to make for his sister Mary Jane in 1845:

> *Mary Jane, my sister, was then a comely girl about sixteen years of age. Indian chiefs offered father fifty horses and a hundred blankets for her; they didn't care whether the girl was willing . . . This was their custom. . . . This scared Mary Jane, and she didn't want to show herself when the Indians were around.*

A sixteen-year-old redheaded beauty named Mary Field had a persistent pursuer in 1852. She and her mother had to resort to deception to get the Indian to leave:

> *[One] Chief took a special fancy to me . . . and offered many ponies for me, but Mother refused. . . . We were all very worried for fear he would steal me so Mother decided to hide me [and] took our feather beds and placed them over two boxes and I crawled under there. Sure enough the Indian Chief came back with his men. He asked for me. Mother told him I was lost. . . . [The] chief stayed with the company all day [and] searched but did not find me. He even felt the feather bed I was under.*

In an interesting turnabout, some young Sioux women, who must have believed in equal rights, "offered six horses for a young emigrant man they fancied" according to one historian. In another switch, John McWilliams had an interesting offer in 1849 along the Blue Mountains in Oregon:

Chief Alikot took quite a fancy to me; he would cross his finger and say: "Sitjum Siwack—half Indian" as I had long black hair and no beard, and was sunburned until I was as dark as an Indian. After we were in camp he made motions that if I would go to his camp & marry his daughter, he would give me one hundred horses. I had to decline his liberal offer, but I never heard the last of it; the boys thought it a good joke on me.

Such offers were no joke to the Indians, however, and some emigrants learned this the hard way. In one company, a man agreed to trade one of the girls to a chief for horses. Catherine Thomas, age nine in 1851, recalled this scene that went from humor to horror:

There was one young chap whose name was Steve Devenish. He was an awfully jolly, likeable chap. All the girls liked him. He was quite a cut-up and great hand at joking. One day some Indians came [and they] were very anxious to get some of the white girls for wives. When Steve found what the chief wanted, he pointed to one of the prettiest girls . . . and asked the chief what he would pay for her. The chief offered ten horses [then] raised his bid to 20 horses. Steve said, "Sold. She's yours." All the girls and young fellows thought this was a great joke. The next day the chief caught up with us and turned 20 head of stock loose and demanded the girl. Steven explained that he was joking.

The Indians were furious and a battle ensued. Several wagons were burned and cattle taken, forcing all the women and children to walk. Steve was banished from the train. "We all felt pretty bad for a few days after Steve left," Catherine remarked. "We hoped he wouldn't fall into the hands of the chief that he played the joke on." (This young man ended up in Idaho, wiser in the ways of Indians.)

Casualties of History

Over time, American expansion into the West brought many changes, most of them bad for the native people. Wagons cut deep ruts through the landscape and cattle depleted the grasses. Wildlife started to disappear, especially the buffalo, upon which the Indians depended for food, shelter, and clothing. Perhaps worst of all, the white people passed on diseases to which Indians had no immunity.

Each year, as the line of emigrant wagons grew longer, the Indians' fears grew that they would be driven completely from their land. By 1849 wagons stretched from Fort Kearny, Nebraska, to Fort Laramie, Wyoming, and beyond. Those headed for the goldfields in California often had too much whiskey and too little patience, and they cared little how they treated the natives.

In addition, some white people felt it necessary to convert the Indians to white society's ways, particularly with regard to religion. Though well intentioned, those people failed to consider the Indians' own wishes and showed little respect for the Indians' traditions and beliefs. The Indians lived in harmony with nature in a way that whites did not understand nor appreciate. Their relationship with the land was one of unity. Nature was their religion, and they considered the earth to be their mother. Most Indians saw no need for another God.

When the Protestant missionaries arrived in Oregon Territory in 1836 and Father Pierre-Jean De Smet first went to the Flathead Mission in 1840, there were rumors that some tribes still performed human sacrifices of young women, and many tribes practiced polygamy. The missionaries wished to persuade the Indians to accept Christian values instead. They had little success at first. They told the Indians that their ways did not please God in heaven, and they would burn in hell if they did not accept this God. It was an image they could not comprehend.

Eventually, however, many Indians did become Christians. Edward Lenox, age sixteen in 1843, recalled a native family he met near Whitman's Station in Oregon. Dr. Whitman had sent the father, named Stickas, to help the emigrants. Edward remembered:

> Stickas had with him his wife and two daughters, and at our evening devotions that night the two girls sang some beautiful hymns, and Stickas himself offered a short prayer.

Becoming friends with the whites and adapting to their ways carried a price, however. Besides giving up their own heritage, the Indians also suffered from diseases they contracted from the emigrants, including smallpox, cholera, and measles. Because they had no natural resistance to these diseases, the Indians died by the thousands. Many pioneers commented on seeing sick and dying natives. Mrs. Lucena Parsons, traveling westward in 1850, left this account:

> We past a camp of Indians today that have the small pox. They have it very bad & many of them have died. We saw one squaw dead under a blanket & her papoose wailing round her [was] sick.

Some white people reflected on what was happening and felt sorry. But for most people in the nineteenth century, the belief in manifest destiny superceded all other considerations. In the end, the Indian way of life was overcome. There were many times more white people than Indian; the Indians were simply outnumbered.

Sara Alexander, a nineteen-year-old who recorded this impression in 1859, was clearly sympathetic to the Indians' plight, though her words reflect the common attitudes of her day:

> The Indians are picturesque and magnificent only in their primitive habitat. . . . I have watched with wonder and delight, as far as the eye could reach, seeing them disappear in the horizon. It is one of the grandest sights my memory recalls . . . . They were my

A Sioux encampment on the Laramie River.
—Courtesy Nebraska State Historical Society

admiration and fear. I pity their humiliation in compelling them to become civilized. So much has to be crushed in the march of improvement and in the making of a nation. . . . I shall always be glad I have seen the Indians in their primitive grandeur.

—SUMMARY—

Most tribes were friendly to the pioneers during the early migration, and many pioneers treated them with friendship in return. As the two peoples got to know each other, mutual fear gave way to curiosity and open exchanges. The trading of goods was beneficial to both parties.

Unfortunately, in spite of this initial goodwill and cooperation, harmonious coexistence was not to be. Most emigrants never learned to totally relax around Indians, and cultural differences continued to cause tension and conflicts. Meanwhile, the white people's diseases devastated the natives, leaving them weakened and grieving. Emigrants and their cattle destroyed the land and wildlife the Indians needed to survive. Ultimately, it was only a matter of time before the Indians were overwhelmed. Yet the Indian people's heritage was not completely destroyed. Many Native Americans and others today work to revive and maintain the cultural traditions nearly lost to history.

Profile of
WELBORN BEESON

Mary Brophy Beeson and Welborn Beeson. —Courtesy of Southern Oregon Historical Society

It was not a common thing for teenage boys to keep diaries in the nineteenth century, but Welborn Beeson was not a common teenage boy. Perceptive and caring, he did his share of the family work and a little more. After tending the fields all day, he helped his mother with the laundry, never protesting that it was "women's work."

John and Ann Beeson, Welborn's parents, emigrated to America from England in about 1830. They lived for a while in New York, then moved to LaSalle County, Illinois. Welborn was born in 1836. He began keeping a diary in 1851, about two years before his family set out on the Oregon Trail.

In 1852 Welborn wrote of an incident that reveals a role he played in the underground railroad as well as his feelings about slavery:

> *May 11. About three I saw a black covered wagon coming to our house. . . . Father [said] it was two young men [who] had brought a runaway Negro on his road to Canada. His name is William Casey. Father wants me to take him to Ottawa tomorrow. . . . Great laws are the laws of America that one part of the people should enslave the rest.*

The Beesons spent over a year preparing for their journey to Oregon. Nearly every day until their departure, Welborn mentions chopping timber, plowing, packing, and buying and selling goods. During their final hectic days in Illinois, they gathered the last of their supplies and said their goodbyes. Excerpts from Welborn's diary describing his experience of the westward trek appear in the chapters of this book.

At the end of the trail, Welborn and his parents settled in Jackson County, Oregon, along Wagner Creek. Their property, which lay about forty miles north of the current California border, is now part of the town of Talent, Oregon. Welborn discovered that their paradise would need a lot of work to tame it. Within a few days of their arrival in late August 1853, he and his father began work on their $1,500 farm: "September 6. We moved to our Farm. . . . We have made 1,000 clapboards to roof a stable. . . . Father and I hauled 5 loads of rails."

Welborn and his father spent about half the month of October splitting rails and breaking prairie. Over the next two years, they built a log cabin schoolhouse near their property, sawing the planks for the desks and benches as well.

While he was on the trail, Welborn had observed the Indians with great fascination and traded with them on occasion. Welborn's father, John, was a believer in Native American rights, and in 1855 he had to flee the country after defending the Indians, insisting they be treated with fairness and equality. He is considered the first civil-rights advocate of Oregon. Welborn, about twenty years old at the time, was pressed into taking full responsibility for the family farm.

Welborn later built another school on the Beeson property. One of the roads meandering through those hills still goes by the name of Beeson Lane. He eventually married Mary Katherine Brophy and had seven children. In about 1862, soon after the beginning of the Civil War, Welborn joined the Union Army.

Welborn lived on the property all his life, nurturing the land, helping his neighbors, and teaching his children. It is little wonder he loved the area. Those who love to fish will appreciate Welborn's enthusiasm for the plentiful salmon in nearby Wagner Creek. On November 24, 1853, about three months after they arrived, he wrote:

I was crossing the creek and saw a very large fish. I waded in and caught it but it was so large that it pushed me down and left me setting in the creek. In the evening I took my rifle and shot two nice sized salmon fish. One was two feet long.

Welborn kept a diary for most of his life. "It will never be read by anyone, and it makes me feel sad," he wrote in 1891, two years before his death. He would no doubt be pleased that so many people find in his writing a remarkable account of the journey to Oregon, and of a young boy who had become a man by the time he arrived.

Welborn died in 1893, at age fifty-seven, and was buried in Sterns Cemetery, not far from his farm. Today, the former Beeson property supports a bountiful pear orchard. Perhaps Welborn even planted some of the trees. Dozens of his descendants in Oregon and other areas are proud to claim Welborn Beeson as their ancestor.

SIX
Romance and Marriage

I certainly can remember vividly the skylarking [flirting] and good times the young folks enjoyed around the camp-fire. . . . Our play games . . . "drop the handkerchief" and "Postoffice," and other kissing games were innocent.

—Remembrance of Catherine Thomas, age ten in 1851

It may be difficult for modern young people, who have free access to sexual information and are indeed surrounded by explicitly sexual messages in the media, to imagine the strict moral attitudes of mid-nineteenth-century culture. The Victorian moral code forbade not only premarital sex but the open discussion of sex. Girls and women wore modest clothing and were expected to behave demurely. Dates were chaperoned, as were parties. If a boy and girl wanted to kiss or even hold hands, they often had to meet in secret. On the trail, however, young people's activities were a bit less supervised than they were back in the states, and due to the rugged conditions, standards of proper behavior were somewhat looser. When teenagers played kissing games like Spin the Bottle, trail parents usually looked the other way.

Still, there were limits to what parents would tolerate. In one Mormon company, some young men were flogged by Hosea Stout, chief of police at Winter Quarters in 1846, for going beyond proper limits with girls there. Stout wrote:

> *They informed [me] that the men had been out with the girls fifteen nights in succession until after two o'clock, and that I should take the matter in hand and see that they had a just punishment by whipping them.*

A young woman's "honor," i.e., virginity, was sacred. A boy who made an improper remark or tried to steal a kiss would likely get slapped. Even if a girl liked a young man, she dare not let him "take advantage." If an unmarried couple was caught having sex, particularly on the frontier, the girl's father or brother might well shoot the boy. A few trail journals and histories mention irate fathers sending young men to their graves for "making too free with" their daughters, and it was generally considered justifiable homicide. Needless to say, pregnancy before marriage was an unspeakable disgrace. If a pregnancy occurred, the male responsible would be compelled to marry the young woman; if that was impossible, the unlucky girl might be forced to marry someone else or simply be sent away.

This commitment to chastity gave rise to a sentimental romanticism about love, courtship, and marriage. When pioneers mentioned such topics, the remarks were often couched in coy references to "Cupid's arrows." Seventeen-year-old Frankie Ward sang a typical love song in 1853:

> *I have something sweet to tell you,*
> *But the secret you must keep,*
> *And remember if it isn't right*
> *I am talking in my sleep.*
> *For I know I am but dreaming*
> *When I think your love is mine,*
> *And I know they are but seeming*
> *All the hopes that round me shine.*

Yet in reality, young women often married men they did not love, in an attempt to escape unhappy lives, to obey their parents' wishes, or because of social pressure. Nevertheless, there were accounts of real romance on the trail, and true love did exist.

Farewell My Love

As the westering wagons moved out, many young sweethearts had to say goodbye, knowing it was most likely forever. Letters to and from frontier homesteads could take months to reach their destination, and visits would be nearly out of the question. One young emigrant, Margaret Judd, later wrote of a tender goodbye scene in 1849, when she was seventeen:

> *The night before we left, my true love, Henry Ridgeley, came to bid me farewell, and under our trysting [courting] tree we each vowed eternal constancy, for four years at least. . . . At the end of that time he would be of age, and then he would come to find me, even if I was at the end of the earth.*

Such promises were seldom kept, however. Life on the trail offered numerous opportunities to make new friends, and old loves were usually forgotten. The end of Margaret's story illustrates the reality:

> *Well, he did come to see me, but it was forty years later and I had a husband and was the mother of thirteen children, he had a wife and three children.*

Most of the married men heading for the gold mines left their wives and children behind. It was considered "unmanly" to be emotional in those days, but many young husbands probably had a lump in their throat as they sang songs like this on the trail:

> *Gather round the campfire and sing a little song*
> *Just to soothe the heart boys, and pass the time along.*

Never count the teardrops, the dearly loved one shed.
Think how sweet the meeting day will be instead.
Sing we of the future, soon, we hope, to come,
When we'll meet the loved ones
In the mountain home.
Never more to sever, while this life shall last
Then in joy we'll bury all the sorrows past.

Even when lovers went west together, sometimes the perils of the trail overtook them and put an end to their happiness. Nancy Hill was a beautiful and talented young woman of about twenty. Nancy and her family were traveling from Missouri to California in 1852 in a wagon party that included Nancy's fiancé, Mr. Wright (we don't know his first name). As one emigrant account described her, "Nancy Hill was a goddess of a girl, six feet tall and magnificently healthy." A historian noted,

> Nancy Hill . . . was loved and honored by all her company, not alone because of her beauty of appearance and character, for in addition to those charms she was an expert hand with horses and oxen and a crack shot with a rifle.

Mr. Wright was totally smitten with her.

Nancy probably contracted cholera on the trail. After a brief illness she died July 5, 1852, at the Sublette Cutoff, near present Kemmerer, Wyoming. Her uncle reported her death in a letter to relatives:

> This day was called on to consign to the tomb one other of our company, N. J. Hill. she was in good health on sunday evening taken unwell that knight, worst in the morning and a corps at nine oclock at knight.

She was buried near the camp.

Nancy's grieving sweetheart stood by her grave and mourned for two days while the other wagons traveled on. Mr. Wright returned three more times to visit the grave of his unforgettable love. On his last visit in 1900, he asked a local citizen to watch over the lonely grave of his Nancy. He must have been in his eighties by then. An iron fence guards the grave today.

The Romance of the Trail

Wherever there are young men and women, there is romance. The still nights under the stars, sharing music, laughter, and tears around a blazing campfire, all the while feeling the uncertainty of what lay ahead—all these things made for a highly dramatic and romantic setting. In 1843 Jesse Applegate, uncle to the youngster of that name, captured this charming trail scene in an article he later wrote:

> *Before a tent near the river a violin makes lively music, and some youth and maidens have improvised a dance upon the green; in another quarter a flute gives its mellow and melancholy notes to the still air. . . . The flute has whispered its last lament to the deepening air and youths have whispered a tender "Good night" in the ears of blushing maidens, or stolen a kiss from the lips of some future bride—for Cupid here as elsewhere [brings] together congenial hearts.*

At Independence Rock, a chivalrous young man might offer to climb up and inscribe a girl's name for her. Many young ladies would not dare to climb up high, lest they reveal a delicate ankle. Mr. Jim Nesmith no doubt impressed the ladies with his gallantry in 1843:

> *I had the satisfaction of putting the names of Miss Mary Zackary and Miss Jane Mills on the southeast point of the rock, near the road, on a high point . . . in all the splendor of gunpowder, tar and buffalo grease.*

117

Trail life was not always conducive to love, however. Albert Jones, sixteen, mentions how cold weather had put a damper on flirting in his 1856 handcart company:

At the first fall of snow, [we felt] a great gloom upon us. We boys that up to this date rendered attentions to the Girls, had our spirits checked to [the] freezing point and the little God Cupid sped off for warmer climes.

Most of the time, though, little could deter ardent young suitors. Because men far outnumbered women on the frontier, few young ladies were allowed to be wallflowers for long. So much male attention could even become tiresome, judging from seventeen-year-old Helen Stewart's comment in 1853, "Me and Agnes are plagued by fellows."

Many romances began on the trail and led to marriage later. Tying the knot with teamsters was commonplace. In 1851 Aurelia Spencer married Thomas Rogers, a teamster in her company, after they arrived in Utah. She was seventeen. "A new life was opening up before me," Aurelia wrote in her autobiography.

Amanda Gardener, a young black slave on the trail in 1853, also found love on the way to Oregon. Teamster Benjamin Johnson married Amanda soon after they reached their destination. Amanda was freed at age twenty but she continued to live and work for her former owners, "for they were my family," she explained. Amanda never had children of her own.

Sisters Helen and Agnes Stewart, "plagued by fellows" in 1853, both married teamsters in their company. Their two other sisters had wed two brothers from a family named Warner. Then Agnes married a third Warner brother! Helen, however, broke the cross-family marrying habit by hitching up with David S. Love in 1855.

Forbidden Fruit

Young Mormons Lucy Marie Canfield, age fifteen, and her cousin Rose found some attentive young men en route to Utah in 1862.

"Sept 28th. Camped near a military station, the soldiers invited us to take dinner with them." Even though it was frowned upon by their elders, some young Mormon women were not afraid to flirt with "gentiles," as the Saints called non-Mormons. According to one diarist, a woman "chastised some sisters for flirting with gentlemen boat passengers who were strangers and not members of the church." In another account in 1860:

> [Some] sisters were reproved for giving encouragement to strangers around camp, and for . . . entering into conversation with gentiles no matter how obscene their language.

The same girls were also reprimanded for attending a dance with soldiers at Fort Bridger. Apparently these girls had a mind of their own when it came to the opposite sex.

The Makings of a Frontier Wife

Many traditional sex roles of the nineteenth century did not hold up well on the frontier. The rugged conditions demanded that women abandon some of the stricter constraints of feminine gentility. In fact, many women embraced the new freedoms and opportunities the West offered, and some went west for just that reason. Marilla Washburn knew how to handle a gun and navigate a canoe, among other things. She was thirteen when she went west with her family in 1852, and she married not long after:

> I was married at 15, and I was not only a good cook and housekeeper, I knew how to take care of babies. . . . I could paddle a canoe, or handle the oars in a rowboat as well as an Indian. I could rustle the meat on which we lived, for I could handle a revolver or rifle as well as most men. I have shot bears, deer, and all sorts of smaller game. During the early days I lived in tents, in log pens, and in log cabins.

Pioneer women and girls herded cattle, hitched up and drove teams, caught fish, and hunted game. Once settled, they also had to help build cabins, make clothes, cook in a fireplace, keep house, plant and tend a garden, and raise children. The stronger and more skilled a young woman was, the more desirable she was as a mate. As one historian noted, "On the trail the men could judge which young woman could build a good fire."

In Oregon, a married man could claim 640 acres of land, but a bachelor could claim only half that amount, so finding a wife was often a priority. That fact combined with the shortage of women on the West Coast meant that any woman wishing to marry had her choice of suitors, regardless of whether or not she could "build a good fire."

It was not uncommon in those days for girls to receive marriage proposals from total strangers. At Fort Laramie an officer asked for the hand of a pretty Mormon girl, Christena McNeil, traveling with a handcart company in 1856. Agnes Caldwell, age nine at the time, was there and remembered the encounter:

> The officer seemed very kind . . . and used the time [that they were unchaperoned] trying to persuade Christena to stay there, proposing to her and showed her the gold he had, telling her what a fine lady he would make of her [but] she told him she would take her chances with the others even though it might mean death. The officer . . . seemed to admire her for her loyalty to her faith and gave her a large cured ham and wished her well in her chosen adventure.

Elizabeth Shepard was just twelve when her family journeyed west in 1852. They settled in northern Oregon. "In the spring of 1853 Father took up for his donation land claim a beautiful, grassy level meadow about two miles west of the Dalles." At age fourteen, Elizabeth married a twenty-eight-year-old man whom she had met only once. The story of this meeting and marriage was typical for those days, especially in places like Oregon, where the distances between settlements were great and the opportunities for young people to meet and court were limited. Elizabeth was with her father and sister on a trip to Vancouver in 1854 when she became betrothed:

When [John Dodd, a man they met on the trip] found out I was upwards of 14 years old, he said he had a friend named Henry Holtgrieve who was looking for a wife [so] on our way back we stopped. Mr. Holtgrieve was there and he and Father talked the matter over and said he would be up the next week to our place to marry me.

Apparently, no one asked Elizabeth what she thought. Together they had a good life, however. "I milked cows and make butter which we sold to the army officers at Fort Vancouver," she said. They had six children.

Wagonside Weddings

Many young pioneer women dreamed of a romantic wedding in a church with a beautiful gown, as they do today, so brides-to-be often postponed their marriages until they could manage these things. Others, however, couldn't wait and got "hitched" alongside the oxen.

The first recorded marriage on the trail was performed in the Bidwell-Bartleson party on June 1, 1841, by Reverend Joseph Williams. He joined in holy matrimony "a couple of young people without law or license." Father Pierre-Jean De Smet married another pair a few weeks later. The couples' names were not recorded.

A trail wedding was usually cause for music, dancing, and special food and drink. It was common practice in those days to disturb young newlyweds right after the ceremony, known as a chivaree. Rebecca Nutting, fourteen at the time, remembered this 1850 wedding years later:

On May 21st David Parker and Catherine Hickman was married.
Such a Chivarie as they got that night was enough to awaken the
Seven Sleepers. The newly married couple occupied a wagon for
sleeping apartments.... [We] took hold of the wagon and the men
at the tongue pulling, the women at the back pushing and ran
the wagon a half mile out on the prairie. Then the fun began.
Such a banging of cans and shooting of guns.... The disturbance
was kept up until midnight.

Another trail wedding was held on top of Independence Rock
on the Fourth of July 1859. Mr. Alden Brooks made these light-
hearted remarks in his diary:

Drove 5 miles to Independence Rock.... After I left a wedding
took place on the rock a grand foundation to get united on. I had
rather get married on the Devil's Gate—which is in sight.

Mary Ann Frost Sterns, nineteen, had a simple wedding when
she married teamster Oscar Winters on the trail in 1852. Mormon
apostle Lorenzo Snow, passing through, performed the ceremony.
Mary Ann recalled that her wedding supper consisted of "baked
bread in a skillet, a piece of meat, and a little lump of fresh butter
with a cup of cold water."

Nineteenth-century girls got prepared for marriage at a young
age. They knew how to keep house by the time they were twelve,
and in many families girls were considered mature and ready to
marry at fifteen, the legal minimum age. Most young women of
that era had a husband before they were twenty. They chose their
husbands mostly on the basis of character and the ability to provide a good living, though love could certainly be a factor. Suitors
were expected to ask the girl's parents for permission to marry,
and some parents chose their daughter's husbands for them. But
most young people wanted to pick out their own mates, and if
their choice did not suit their families, the couple sometimes eloped.

One young woman in 1852 was determined not to let her boyfriend leave for Oregon without her:

Boone Johnson got a job driving across the plains. . . . I was nearly 16 and we had been going together [and] decided to get married but my father refused permission. He said we were both too young.

The future Mrs. Johnson's sister and brother happened to be leaving for Oregon with the same wagon train, the Reverend Joab Powell's company. It was a chance to elope:

When the train pulled out, I joined it. I wanted Mr. Powell to marry us. He said he couldn't on the east side of the Missouri, but when we got out on the plains, he would. We were married on May 3, with more than 500 people at our wedding [and] an honest to goodness wedding cake. My husband drove a wagon and I did the cooking to pay my way.

In 1855 a twenty-year-old Englishman named Stephen Forsdick, a former Mormon, was on his way to Fort Laramie when he met and fell in love with seventeen-year-old Mormon Lucinda Melissa Davenport. Melissa (she went by her middle name) was traveling back to Council Bluffs from Utah with her brother. Stephen proposed, and Melissa accepted even though her brother disapproved of Stephen. Melissa continued on to Council Bluffs, 525 miles away from Fort Laramie, and the sweethearts sadly parted.

A year later Stephen learned that Melissa was returning to Utah and would be camping near Fort Laramie. He arranged a romantic "kidnapping" of his lady love. After nightfall a friend came for Melissa at her camp and they hurried to the fort, but not without being seen. The men in her company gave chase, but she reached the fort before they caught up with her, and they could not get her back because she was now under government protection. The fort chaplain married Melissa and Stephen on October 2, 1856. "We never regretted getting married," Stephen said years later.

One trail wedding in 1859 seemed like a twist of fate. A young man who had left his fiancée in England the year before was heading east with a wagon train as his lady love was heading west, each unbeknownst to the other. The two companies met at Independence Rock. Mr. William Atkin, in the young woman's camp, wrote about this lucky encounter in his autobiography:

> Out of curiosity, he [came] to see [our] handcart company camped nearby. There he found his sweetheart, and her parents, who at once made arrangements for the marriage.

The captain of the bride's company performed the wedding, with the Sweetwater River and Independence Rock as an enchanting backdrop.

Not all trail weddings were so heartwarming. Mr. William Atkin observed this less-than-romantic episode in the same handcart company later that year. As the exhausted and nearly starving company was camped near a mail station at the Big Sandy River in Wyoming, some rough-looking mountain men approached. What happened next was a shock, according to Mr. Atkin:

> [Two] mountain men, with more whiskey than good sense . . . stepped out of the house and yelled: "We want to get a wife, who wants to marry?" To the great surprise of those in the camp, two of our young women stepped out and they said they would marry them. One of the young women had a [boyfriend] in our company, but alas, the starving conditions seemed to drive all natural feelings away from them. There were two weddings celebrated that day in the mountains.

—SUMMARY—

Whether the relationships ended in marriage, like that of Stephen Forsdick and Melissa Davenport, or tragedy, like that of Mr. Wright and his Nancy, or just plain ended, like that of Margaret Judd and her "true love," there was plenty of romance on the Emigrant Trail. It must have made the trip much more interesting for the young pioneers to think about an attractive girl or boy sleeping in the next tent or wagon. Yet actual contact between the sexes was carefully supervised.

Courtship was chaste, and brides were young (and often so were grooms). Girls had to become well prepared at an early age for the rugged life of a frontier wife. Yet they could be choosy about whom to marry. Young men had to beat out a lot of competition if they wanted to win a lady's hand.

After getting their parents' approval, a young pair could marry. Engaged couples on the trail who wanted a nice church ceremony had to wait until they reached Utah, California, or Oregon. For the less patient, a prairie wedding with music, dancing, and a wagon "chivarie" could be even more romantic.

Profile of
ABIGAIL SCOTT (DUNIWAY)

Abigail Scott (Duniway).
—Courtesy Oregon Historical Society

When Abigail Jane Scott was born to John Tucker and Ann Roclofson Scott in Tremont, Illinois, on October 22, 1834, no white woman—and only a few white men—had even seen the Oregon country. Abigail was to become Oregon's leading feminist as well as a famous author.

On April 1, 1852, at the age of seventeen, Abigail left Illinois with her parents and eight siblings, bound for Oregon and opportunity. Abigail's family appointed her the record keeper for the journey. The writing of her journal imprinted the events on her mind for years:

Our family, consisting of eleven persons, started across the plains with five wagons, twenty-one yoke of cattle and one span of horses. . . . There is in my possession now a battered, time-stained, ink-bespattered diary, kept during that six months' journey. . . . Today as I turn its battered pages and read between its lines, I am a child again.

Abigail's mother—"our gentle, faithful, self-sacrificing mother"—died of cholera a few weeks after they left for Oregon. That year was the worst for cholera deaths on the trek west. Abigail caught the disease and recovered, but her little brother Willie, age four, also died before the journey ended.

Although Abigail had little formal education, she taught school her first year in Oregon. After her marriage a year later to Ben C. Duniway, she stopped teaching and took on the duties of a wife and, soon, of a mother. Abigail's life became what she called a "general pioneer drudge."

Besides caring for her own family—she had six children in all—Abigail served as cook and all-purpose maid to several men who worked for her husband. She entertained visitors by reading her early attempts at writing. Many of these were published in nearby Oregon City's newspaper, the *Argus*. Abigail's first pieces did not bring any financial rewards, but they helped her achieve a bit of fame:

> *I wrote up my experiences to read to my rustic neighbors, in fashion primitive enough, heaven knows, for I was without education and had no knowledge of the simplest rudiments of what the world calls literature. . . . Many were the neighbors from miles away who would come to our cabin to hear [my] pieces read or sent their children on horseback to borrow the paper.*

Farm chores came first. In addition to caring for her family, Abigail made hundreds of pounds of butter and collected eggs to sell at the market for extra money. Still, she found moments in which to write her stories.

Then bad judgment or bad luck cost the Duniways their farm: Ben cosigned some bank notes for a friend who could not pay his debts. Soon afterward, an accident left Ben an invalid, and Abigail was forced to support the family. Perhaps life on the trail helped prepare Abigail for these challenges. She taught school again, then went into business, moving her family to Albany, Oregon, where opportunities were more plentiful. Abigail opened a millinery and notions store. Still, despite her many duties as breadwinner and mother, she found time to write two novels based on their trail journey, *Captain Grey's Company* and *From West to West*.

In talking with her customers, Abigail realized how much women worked and how few rights they had under the law. At home, she fumed about the injustice. Ben finally said, "Don't you know it will never be any better for women until they have the right to vote?" Abigail had to agree. "The idea filled me with such hope, courage, and determination as no obstacle could conquer and nothing but death could overcome."

Abigail began to advocate equal rights for women to any willing listener. Irate men yelled at her for going beyond a "woman's sphere." Undaunted, she persevered, loved by many, feared by some, and hated by those who did not want "women to become men." Her final appeal for equal rights, made to Oregon voters in the late nineteenth century, remains a monument to her efforts:

> *It is nearly forty-two years since I, an inexperienced tyro in public affairs, began laying the foundation for equal suffrage. I am an old woman now. . . . I do not myself expect ever to be able to cast a full free ballot, but I do hope that you gentlemen who have never been*

compelled to struggle for the right to vote will vote 300 [times].
Yes and send me to heaven as a free angel.

Abigail did live to "cast a full free ballot" in Oregon, though she did not live to see suffrage for all American women. Thanks to her efforts, Oregon women won their voting rights in 1912. In October 1915, 25,000 women marched on New York City, demanding the right to vote. Five years later, women all over the country were finally able to cast a ballot. Several books have been written about Abigail; others have featured her as a major player in the suffrage movement. Abigail died in 1915 at the age of eighty.

SEVEN

Danger, Disease, and Death

The ruthless monster death, not yet content has once more entered our fold & taken in his icy grip the treasure of our hearts! Last night our darling Willie [her little brother] was called from earth, to vie with angels around the throne of God.

—Diary of Abigail Jane Scott, age seventeen, 1852

The earliest pioneers may have had little idea of the hazards that lay ahead, but tales soon spread of Indian massacres, starvation, disease, accidents, and lost children. Though the risk of Indian attacks was rather exaggerated, the dangers of the trail were very real.

The worst thing that could happen to any westering family was to have to leave a loved one (or several) buried in the wilderness. On the trail, death could come from wagon accidents, poisoning, getting caught in stampedes, drowning, freezing, starvation, exhaustion, disease, and even murder. Many children were orphaned on the trail, and some parents lost all their children.

Caught under the Wheels

Families with a wagon and team had a big survival advantage over the poorer handcart emigrants—the draft animals bore the burden, and the wagon supplied extra shelter and storage for supplies. But wagon wheels, enemies of young children, caused a surprising number of deaths and near-deaths on the trail.

Headstone of Joel Hembree. —Courtesy Randy Martin

Nine-year-old Joel Hembree had the unwanted distinction of being the first wagon-wheel casualty on the Oregon Trail. He fell underneath a wheel on July 18, 1843, and lingered one day before death claimed him. A family friend carved his name and the date on a large stone by his grave. In 1961 a rancher discovered the grave and gave Joel a place in history. He reburied the remains in a pine box and held a ceremony witnessed by interested spectators. The original marker still guards this grave.

Catherine Sager, age ten, was another early victim of a wagon-wheel accident in 1844:

> *The children had become so accustomed to getting in and out of the wagon as to lose all fear, and would get out on the tongue and leap clear of the wheel without putting Father to the trouble of stopping the team. . . . In performing this feat, the hem of my dress caught on an axe-handle, precipitating me under the wheels, both of which passed over me, badly crushing the left leg. . . . That accident confined me to the wagon for the remainder of the journey.*

It took more than a year for her leg to heal.

In 1846 the traffic westward increased dramatically, and so had trail accidents. On June 6 of that year, Mr. Nicholas Carringer noted this accident in his diary:

> This day traveled 9 miles one boy [Enoch Garrison] fell and two wheels run over one leg and the other foot and ancle nearly Cutting the leg off, breaking the bone so it injured the other foot and Ancle and We encamped for the day.

A week later seven-year-old Enoch had received no medical attention. Mr. Edwin Bryant, an emigrant in a nearby company who had a reputation for doctoring, was called to help. Mr. Bryant left this graphic account:

> When I reached the tent . . . and examined the wound for the first time, it was discovered that gangrene had taken place, and the limb of the child was swarming with maggots I told [the mother] all efforts to save him would be useless, and would only add to the anguish of which he was now dying. A Canadian Frenchman . . . stated he had formerly assisted a doctor [and he] would amputate the leg.

Mr. Bryant could not stand to watch the agony of this procedure. Enoch was given laudanum, a tincture of opium used to ease pain, but it had little effect, and he died before the Frenchman had finished. Mr. Bryant wrote that night that, after attending a wedding, he "saw the procession of the little boy to his last resting-place, [and it] produced sadness and depression."

The first wagon-wheel death on the Mormon exodus from Winter Quarters, Nebraska, in 1847 was probably that of six-year-old Robert R. Gardner. According to diarist Mr. James Smithies, father of a family in the same company, Robert was buried "on the west side of the Black Hills exact half a mile from the Bank of the Platte river." He died in the same region and of the same cause as Joel Hembree four years earlier.

Quick thinking saved some other children from a similar fate. Susan Woodruff, age eight, had a near miss with the wheels of her family's wagon. According to the journals of her father, Wilford Woodruff:

> Rhoda [Susan's grown cousin] was knocked out of the Carriage & Susan was lying flat upon the bottom with her feet hanging out between the wheels and she was screaming aloud. I [yelled] for her to hold on untill I [could] come. She did so until I caught the Horse by the bit and stoped him & rescued her.

Charley True, sixteen during his 1859 journey to California, saved his little sister from a death under the wheels. He wrote this account in his memoirs almost fifty years later:

> I was taking a turn at driving our team and frequently looked miles across the country at Fort Kearney. Suddenly, I turned at my mother's terrified call to see the near forward wheel passing over the leg of my four year old sister, Carro who had fallen out of the wagon. By acting promptly I dragged her from the pathway of the hind wheel, which would have passed over her head, killing her or leaving her in a condition far worse than death.

Carro, her leg injured, rode the rest of the way in the wagon, comforted by her brother's dog Prince. She eventually recovered.

According to the 1847 diary of thirteen-year-old Jesse N. Smith, miracles could also heal a wagon-wheel victim:

> I recollect one day that a large heavily loaded wagon ran over one of Brother Pratt's little boys, about two years old; he took up the child and laid hands on him [and blessed him] and the child never complained, and soon was as well as before to all appearance.

Water Hazards

Drowning was a common cause of death among the pioneers. Rivers were especially dangerous when the water was high. Freezing water, boiling hot springs, and boat accidents also took their toll.

In 1843 in an Oregon-bound company from Missouri headed by his uncle, seven-year-old Jesse Applegate lost two cousins and one brother in the Columbia River, toward the end of their journey. The accident stayed with young Jesse:

At the head of the rapids, the river bares from a west course. . . . The boat began to rise and fall and rock from side to side. . . . The persons in this boat were Alexander McClennan . . . William Parker and three boys, Elisha Applegate, aged about eleven, and Warren and Edward Applegate, each about nine years old. . . . Presently there was a wail of anguish, a shriek, and a scene of confusion. . . . The boat disappeared and we saw the men and boys struggling in the water.

The witnesses could only stand by as the water—too dangerous to enter—took the three boys and Mr. McClennan. The same year on the same river, lawyer Peter Burnett's "young servant girl" was sent after a bucket of water and was apparently swept away by a strong wave. She was never seen again.

Seven-year-old Eliza Ann Grover and others nearly drowned in a bizarre accident at Nauvoo in February 1846. The Grover family was crossing the river on a barge when a young man, apparently practicing his spitting technique, took careless aim with a mouthful of tobacco juice. The juice went into the eye of an ox, causing the animal to bolt and a wagon to overturn. Several men jumped in to rescue some of the people thrown overboard. Meanwhile Eliza Ann—as her sister Emmeline, age fifteen at the time, later described—saved the life of a baby:

My sister Eliza Ann who was about seven and a babe six months old [fell] as the wagon was pitched down into the water. She immediately plunged down, caught the babe by his dress by one hand while she used the other to help her climb back up with her head out of the water holding the babe.

The worst water disaster of the Mormon migration occurred in 1852 on the Missouri River near Lexington, Missouri, when the steamboat *Saluda* exploded, wounding or killing about a hundred people. The river was clogged with ice that day, and the boat was making slow progress. In an attempt to make up time, the captain overheated the engines. Most passengers were still in bed when the explosion occurred. One father later wrote this chilling narrative:

I was blown into the river by the explosion. . . . I looked around and saw the mangled form of a child lying close by me. Recognizing its clothing I soon made the startling discovery that it was my own dear baby boy, whom I, a short time before, had seen in its mothers arms.

Steamboat engines were finnicky and explosions were not uncommon. There were many other kinds of boat accidents as well. A little boy on board the *Charles Buck* in 1855 got entangled in the ropes of the ship and was thrown overboard. In 1865 another little boy on a boat fell through a trap door that had been left open.

Sometimes hot springs that looked inviting were in fact deadly hot. Many animals died in the sulfuric hot springs near the end of the Humboldt Sink in Nevada, particularly dogs and oxen, and humans were also injured there. On September 4, 1852, seventeen-year-old Eliza Ann McAuley wrote about these treacherous waters:

These springs boil up with great noise, emitting a very nauseous smell. . . . We hear that a woman and child have got scalded very badly by stepping into one of them.

Fatal Mistakes

Hazards lurked everywhere on the trail, and some deaths could have been avoided with a little more caution. In the early 1860s, eighteen-year-old Caroline Todd and three other young women climbed to the top of the ridge at Devil's Gate, in central Wyoming, where Caroline became part of trail history by falling to her death. Her family buried her in the gorge near two other graves.

Accidental poisonings also occurred. In 1846 five-year-old Lettie Henderson died after drinking from a bottle of laudanum that hung on a nail in her wagon. Many families carried this tonic for pain and to treat many ailments; doctors recommended it for Rocky Mountain fever and cholera. It was not a habit in those days to keep medicines under lock and key. Lettie's sister Lucy, age eleven in 1846, was in the wagon with her friend, fourteen-year-old

Devil's Gate.
—Author photo

Elizabeth Currier, at the time of this incident, which she recounted many years later:

> I shall never forget that camp. Mother had brought some medicine along [laudanum]. . . . My playmate, the Currier girl and I decided to taste the medicine. . . . My little sister, Salita Jane [Lettie] wanted to taste but I told her she couldn't. When mother called her for supper she didn't come. When mother tried to awake her later she couldn't arouse her. Lettie had drunk the whole bottle of laudanum. It was too late to save her life. Three days later after my little sister Lettie died, my sister Olivia was born.

Elizabeth was so moved by the tragedy that she "cut a beaded flower from her bag and laid it on the grave."

Emigrants had to be especially careful around campfires. Catherine Sager wrote in her memoir of the near death of her sister in 1844:

> We arrived at Grand Round somewhere near the last of September. While encamped there one of my sisters caught fire, and would have burned to death had it not been for the timely aid of the Doctor. His hands were much burned in extinguishing the flames.

Boiling water was another campground hazard. Two sisters waiting for their supper at Devil's Gate in 1850 got rambunctious and the younger child, age three, fell backwards into a pot of boiling water. Her screams echoed all around the camp and the adults rushed to the scene. The girl was not expected to live, but she did eventually recover. Another youngster was not so lucky. The boy's sister, Emma Perkins, who was not yet born when her family crossed the plains, was told about her brother's horrible death:

> My brother Jerry C. Perkins was a little chap when he crossed the plains. He was playing with a rope and tripped on the rope and

fell into the campfire, knocking over a large kettle of boiling water, which scal[d]ed him to death.

"Natural" Causes

Nature often proved deadly for the pioneers. On July 15, 1850, Miss Sophia Goodridge, in the Wilford Woodruff company, wrote in her journal that lightning claimed the life of a young man near Fort Kearny, Nebraska. Six years later, fourteen-year-old James Stoddard lived through a lightning strike when his handcart company was caught in a thunderstorm on the Nebraska plains. Mr. Archer Walters captured the July 26, 1856, scene:

Traveled about 6 miles. As soon as we crossed [Loup Fork] it looked dark and black. . . . it began to lightning and soon the thunder roared and about the middle of the trail of handcarts the lightning struck a brother and he fell to rise no more in that body. . . . One boy [who was] burned a little was named James Stoddard: we thought he would die but he recovered and was able to walk, and Brother Wm. Stoddard, father of the boy was knocked to the ground.

In 1849 Mr. J. Goldsborough Bruff recorded a horrible scene of death by an "act of God" in his diary. Mr. Bruff, hearing loud screams and hurrying to investigate, discovered a father and two sons crushed by a fallen tree: "Oct 31. We raised the blood-stained tent [and] there lay a shocking sight." Mr. Bruff performed the burials later that day and inscribed the grave marker: "Ormond Alford, aged 54 yrs. and his sons—William M., aged 19 and Lorenzo D., aged 15 years. Killed by the falling of an oak tree."

Pioneers from eastern cities often came west with a fear of the beasts in the wilderness. While a few emigrants died of snakebite and some were killed in buffalo stampedes, overall, wild animals posed a relatively minor threat. Animals such as bears, wolves, and coyotes were more likely to attack the livestock than the pioneers themselves. In fact, the emigrants ran a greater risk of harm from accidents involving their own animals. Many children had arms and legs broken by kicks from oxen, and some died in stampedes under heavy cattle hooves. A young boy in one company got tangled in a horse's rope and was dragged to his death.

Hunger and Thirst

"There is now great suffering from hunger among the emigrants," John Steele, eighteen, wrote on September 14, 1850. "Those who have but a morsel of food daily find it necessary to divide that morsel with someone who has none." In the early years along the Oregon and California routes, so many were starving that settlers sent provisions out to help travelers in trouble.

Many emigrants relied on their ability to dig, forage, and hunt for food. Fourteen-year-old Edwin Pettit described his company's efforts to avoid starvation in 1848:

> During this time, we had to depend upon my brother-in-law, who was a pretty good gunman, as it was very hard for us to get [food] and occasionally he would bring in a quail or wild duck. Many a time we have had to depend on thistle roots or pig weed as our bill of fare.

Thirst was even more life threatening than hunger. In the desert regions, water was worth its weight in gold. Some emigrants claimed they paid fifteen dollars a glassful for water in Nevada, brought in by enterprising predecessors. One account by writer George R. Stewart said emigrants "reported talking with people who had paid a hundred dollars for a pint of water." Even when there was water along the trail, it was often bad. Sarah Moulding, who was only three at the time, recalled in her autobiography the agony of thirst:

> When we did stop to get a drink I would always have to wait until my sister had her drink [because] the older child was always favored and came first in everything. I can remember how I

would dance up and down waiting for her to finish ... and how thirsty I was. The water was warm and never very good. And at times the water was terrible because they would have to dig a hole to get it, and then it would be muddy.

Along parts of the trail, the emigrants never knew when, where, or even if they would find water. The little water there was in the desert was so alkali it was hardly potable. Elisha Brooks, eleven at the time, remembered his company's suffering as they traversed Nevada's salt flats in 1852:

With a lean and worn out team at the tail end of the procession we entered the alkali tracts, only to find the pasturage eaten up, dried up, and burned up, and the August sun ... beat down on the brackish alkali pools from which we must often drink or die of thirst.

Eliza Donner, not yet four years old in 1847, later described how her family dealt with their terrible thirst when crossing the desert:

Disappointment intensified our burning thirst and my good mother gave [us] moistened peppermint and later put a flattened bullet in each child's mouth to engage its attention and help keep the salivary glands in action.

In Iowa and Nebraska there were rivers, but the water was full of mud and "wiggle worms" (probably mosquito larvae). Tea strainers could remove some of the worms but could not get the mud out. One pioneer wrote that she usually "got a pint of mud from a bucket of [river] water." According to twelve-year-old Mary Powell, "Some [children] would suck the water from the mud. The children drank heartily, straining it through their teeth." If they had enough food supplies, emigrants sometimes got mud out of the water by straining it through cornmeal and eggs.

Eliza Donner (Houghton).
—Courtesy California State Library

Of course, it was not only emigrants who suffered on the frontier. Native Americans often died from starvation as well. Benjamin Bonney, age eight, and his parents were traveling from California to Oregon in 1846 when they came upon a pitiful sight:

The young man who took the horses out ... found near the lake an Indian girl about 8 years old. This little girl was perfectly nude, her long black hair was matted, and she was covered with sores from head to feet. She could make only a pitiful moaning sound. Dr. Truman Bonney ... examined her and said she was suffering from hunger and that the flies had almost eaten her up. Nearby we could see where two tribes had fought. She had apparently been left [and] been living on clover and roots and grass.

Benjamin's mother and aunt did all they could to comfort the child, but they could not take her with them. When they started on "the women were in tears." One man took his gun and finally put the little girl out of her misery. It was not uncommon for people to perform "mercy killings" in those days.

Devastating Diseases

On the trail, unsanitary conditions and malnutrition made illness inevitable. The year 1846 was particularly disastrous for groups heading westward. Hundreds of Mormons, many of them children, died of disease that summer, fall, and winter in Iowa and Nebraska. The afflictions included scurvy, "ague and fever" (malaria), cholera, pneumonia, scarlet fever, whooping cough, and others. Sometimes bodies mounted so quickly that they were laid under tents, attended by women keeping flies off them until the few healthy men left could dig enough graves. Sometimes more than one body was buried in a grave.

Before she left Winter Quarters, Nebraska, after the hard winter of 1846–47, fifteen-year-old Ann Cannon paid a final pilgrimage to the cemetery:

> A great many people died with scurvy; a great many were on crutches. Parts of many families died, some parents died. I went with some girls and counted the graves on the hill at Winter Quarters before we left. There were hundreds of them.

In 1852 the family of Elisha Brooks was stricken with measles. He painted this bleak scene in his recollections:

> A picture lingers in my memory of us children all lying in a row on the ground in our tent, somewhere in Iowa, stricken with the measles, while six inches of snow covered all the ground and the trees were brilliant with icicles.

The Brooks children eventually recovered and arrived safely in California.

Cholera, an often fatal intestinal disease, followed early emigrants westward, and by 1850 the fear of it had swept across the country. Cholera came mostly from water contaminated by human waste. In confined spaces such as crowded ships, it could spread very quickly. Forty-five passengers on the steamboat *Berlin* died of cholera in 1849; fifteen were children. In 1850, out of a group of 240 Mormons, 58 on the *Mary* died of cholera and were buried along the banks of the Missouri River.

The disease killed swiftly. A brother and sister in a company camped near John Steele in 1850 died at Heber Springs, in present-day Wyoming. John recorded the scene of mourning:

> *This morning Henry and Louisa Williams, the two stricken with cholera yesterday were buried. The young lady died about midnight, and her brother lingered until dawn. A deep, wide grave was prepared, in which the bodies were laid, coffinless, to mingle with the clay. The parents and another son gazed upon the scene in silent . . . grief.*

In 1854 several hundred Mormons, many from Switzerland, were camped at Mormon Grove, near Fort Leavenworth, Kansas, when cholera attacked. It was a grim, swift scene of death for little Eliza Graehl. Eliza was playing with her dolls one moment, dead the next. Eliza's mother left this account:

> *They made a fine coffin of black walnut and six young ladies of our company carried my lost treasure to her final resting place. . . . We made a wreath of wild grape leaves.*

In that same camp was Jean Frederick Loba, age eight, with his parents and siblings. Jean later recalled:

> *Impressed with the solemnity and the sadness which brooded over us all, we [boys] pledged each other not to surrender. . . but hardly*

had we made a vow, when the youngest of the Stroudemann boys was gone, stricken and buried at [Mormon] Grove.

Some managed to survive cholera. Abigail Scott was one. Her mother and brother died of the disease in 1852. Another survivor was Marilla R. Washburn, age thirteen, whose mother knew a folk remedy:

Two days before we came to Chimney Rock the cholera struck us. Seven died in our train that night and four the next day. A young man in our wagon train named Hyde went out as a guard for the stock that night. When he left, he seemed perfectly well. When the guard was changed at midnight Mr. Wood brought his body back to the train. My brother and I took the cholera. Mother gave us all the hot whiskey she could pour down us and put flannel cloths soaked in whiskey . . . on our stomachs. This cured us.

Marilla's company had barely buried their cholera victims when illness again invaded the camp: "Just after the Fourth of July some of the members of our train took smallpox and four died of it."

Some pioneers died from unnamed or unknown causes. Hosea Stout Jr. died on July 28, 1846, "troubled with evil spirits," according to his father. Mr. J. Goldsborough Bruff, who later buried the victims of a fallen tree, found himself digging a grave for an abandoned four-year-old boy. A man Mr. Bruff later called an "inhuman wretch" heading for the mines had dumped his little son William Lambkin, who had inconveniently become ill, at Bruff's camp in November 1849. The boy cried constantly, then grew melancholy, pale, and quiet. On December 30 Mr. Bruff wrote in his journal:

Found the boy unusually still, chopped a piece of beef small, stewed & thickened it with flour, and on taking it to him, found him just recovering from a fit. Occasioned probably by the state of his stomach. . . . Child's illness increasing, I endeavored to feed him with a little broth.

The child soon died, and Mr. Bruff inscribed the headstone: "William—Infant Son of Lambkin—an Unnatural Father. Died Jan. 1, 1850."

Consumption (tuberculosis), a common nineteenth-century disease, drove some people west, hoping that the dry, temperate climate would cure it. In 1853 Louisa Lithgow, seventeen, was "wasting away with consumption" when her parents decided to make the desperate journey to California to try to restore her health. She got only about halfway. Her teenage cousin, Sarah Louise Hays, recorded Louisa's final words and the tender death scene:

Wasted by a mere shadow of her once radiant self . . . she lay back in the arms of her father her large appealing eyes looking to her fathers face with a last fond look. "O papa. . . Bury me where the wolves can not get me." The large eyes closed—the faint breath fluttered and [she] was gone.

Lost Souls

Many children, some adults, and even whole companies were lost on the trail. In the confusion of a large group—whether a wagon train or a handcart company—children were easily separated from their family, usually temporarily, but sometimes permanently. Because of the unknowns in the wilderness, parents suffered greatly when a child could not be found.

A little boy named Robert, traveling under the guardianship of Margaret Frink in 1850, was missing one night. Mrs. Frink's anguish was captured in her diary:

July 27. Our boy Robert took up a horse near the road, it having the appearance of being lost, and by so doing got separated from us. . . . I suffered the agony almost of death in a few minutes. I be-

144

sought [the people] to turn back and help us look for our lost boy, but they had not time. . . . Never can I forget those minutes. . . . But just at dark, Aaron [a man traveling with them] came in sight, having the lost boy with him. My joy turned into tears.

In large families, parents could not always keep track of all their children. Mrs. Amelia Stewart Knight was traveling to Oregon in 1853 with her husband and their seven children, who were all under the age of sixteen. On August 8 they stopped at Fort Boise, on Idaho's Snake River, then continued on. Mrs. Knight recorded this close call in her journal:

Here we unknowingly left our Lucy [age eight] behind, not a soul had missed her until we had gone some miles. . . . Then another train drove up behind us with Lucy. She was terribly frightened and so were we.

Elisha Brooks recalled a tragic lost-child story that was all too common in emigrant trains:

In one of these camps, a little three year old boy, the only child of his doting parents, was missing at supper time, and we all turned out exploring the country far and near. . . . We found no trace of him. Soon after dark a terrific storm arose . . . destroying all hopes of finding the child alive. . . . All but our family, hitched up and drove on — our teamster with them — leaving the stricken parents alone in their despair.

As this story shows, emigrant companies sometimes abandoned the lost, the grief-stricken, and the sick on the trail. This seemingly heartless practice was believed to be for the greater good. Mr. Carl J. Fields, traveling through Wyoming with a handcart company, noted this episode on September 11, 1860:

> *Here we picked up a poor family which had been left by a former company on account of two very sick children. . . . [Eleven days later] Here the fourteen-year-old daughter of the family we had picked up at Green River, died, and was buried.*

Many journals recorded macabre stories of company members digging graves for people who were not even dead yet; other accounts told of the sick being dumped into graves while they were still alive. In 1859 sixteen-year-old Fanny Fry wrote of nearly being buried alive. She had passed out from exhaustion while pulling a heavy handcart up a steep hill. "When I came to, I was in a tent. . . . The sisters had sewed me up to the waist in my blanket, ready for burial." The men in the company had already started digging a grave for her.

Murder and Justice

Not all trail deaths were caused by disease or accidents. Greed, short tempers, and "frontier justice" resulted in their share of deaths. In addition, though accounts of Indian attacks were often exaggerated, the natives did kill a few emigrants. Thirteen-year-old Jesse N. Smith, who joined the Mormon exodus of 1847, wrote in his journal of a murder during a Pawnee cattle raid on June 19:

> *Our companies rendevoued at the Elk Horn River. . . . Parley P. Pratt and Jacob Weatherby started back to Winter Quarters on business with a pair of steers, a wagon and two women [and] were attacked by three Indians. . . . Weatherby was killed. His body was brought back and buried at the foot of the Liberty Pole, which had been raised in camp.*

The Liberty Pole marked the gathering place for early Mormon pioneers. Twenty-year-old Jacob Weatherby was the first Mormon death at the hands of Indians.

Several accounts of trail experiences report murders by fellow travelers. John Steele encountered a suspicious scene west of Devil's Gate in 1850, but he found it wiser not to pursue justice:

Here we found a wagon in the shade of which lay a young man suffering from fever [and] he told us that he had been sick over a week, and believed two men traveling companions [who were away] intended to kill him, and thus obtain his outfit . . . [Soon the men returned] and bawled out, "Come Hank, tumble into the wagon."

The men's manner was so gruff that John believed that the sick young man's fears were justified. He hurried over the next day with his pistol and a friend and asked for the young man. The traveling companions pointed to a fresh grave. "He lies there," they said. John continued:

Their features and manners indicated guilt. Still he was beyond all human help, and we could only leave them to settle the matter with their final Judge.

Abigail Scott described two markers she saw at Devil's Gate that must have sent a chill down her spine:

[One marker said] "Charles Botsford, murdered June 28th 1852. The murderer lies in the next grave . . . hung June 29th 1852." The other bears the inscription: "Horace Dolley hung June 29th 1852." It appears Dolley had contracted a grudge towards Botsford with regard to some little difficulty between them [and] while alone with him he dealt the blow.

The difficulties of travel guaranteed some shortness of temper. Whether this escalated into rage may have depended more on the parties involved than on the circumstances. Welborn Beeson, seventeen, witnessed a crime of passion in 1853:

June 17. Charly Hepp accidentally struck the mule of a drover by the name of Gregory. Gregory threatened to shoot him. . . . When Charly was not looking, [he] struck him from behind and knocked him senseless. . . . June 19. Charles Hepp died, Killed by one Gregory, a drover from Ohio who is still at large.

If a criminal was caught, trail justice could be swift and severe. At least one teenage boy was condemned to death by his companions. Mr. Henry Allyn, California-bound in 1853, wrote: "In camp, a teen-ager was hanged by a drumhead court for allegedly committing an axe murder." Another diarist, Dr. Samuel Matthias Ayers, made this terse comment in 1850: "A man shot a youth who crept in with his daughter."

—SUMMARY—

According to historians, about 400,000 people migrated westward between 1841 and 1868, and about 10 percent of them died. Over one-half of those deaths were infants and small children. Causes of death ranged from ordinary measles to freak accidents to murder. In a way, it seems remarkable that so many escaped "the ruthless monster death."

Certainly it was a rare company that did not experience some danger, disease, or death, yet the rewards of reaching their goal were, for most emigrant families, worth the risks. In fact, the difficult and tragic experiences seemed only to make the young pioneers stronger. Both while on the trail and later in life, these sturdy young people overcame their personal tragedies to play an active part in settling the Wild West.

Profile of
THE DONNER AND REED CHILDREN

VIRGINIA E. REED.

(Mrs. J. M. Murphy)

Virginia Reed (Murphy).
—Courtesy California State Library

When they started off for California from Springfield, Illinois, on April 16, 1846, the Donner-Reed company of more than eighty emigrants and teamsters had high hopes and plentiful supplies. Both the Donners and the Reeds were wealthy families, and they brought with them many large, well-stocked wagons and dozens of magnificent animals. One of the wagons, which James Reed built especially for his ailing mother-in-law, was dubbed "the Pioneer Palace Car." It had a second-story bedroom, spring seats, a library of books, a big mirror, and a side entrance. Twelve-year-old Virginia Reed rode a handsome pony.

George Donner, head of the party, was sixty-two and had left his grown children in Illinois. With him were Tamsen Donner, his third wife; their three girls, Frances, Georgiana, and Eliza, ages six, four, and three; and two older children from Mr. Donner's second marriage. James Reed and his wife, Margaret, were accompanied by their four children: Virginia, twelve; Martha, who they called Patty, eight; James Jr., five; and Thomas, three. Mrs. Reed's mother also came, but she died during the journey.

At Fort Bridger in Wyoming, the group met up with trail guide Lansford Hastings, who proposed they take a new shortcut he had devised. Some people in the party had misgivings about the untried route, but most were eager to save as much time as Hastings claimed they would, and they decided to take the cutoff.

After Hastings's original plan failed, they tried a different way, but it put them seriously behind schedule. By the time the party arrived in the Sierra Nevada, violent winter storms had already set in, trapping them in the mountains. As members of the group began to die of cold and starvation, the emigrants began to eat rawhide, bark, twigs, grass, and even shoelaces. Eventually they resorted to cannibalism, eating the bodies of the dead.

Nearly half of the eighty-one stranded were children under fifteen years old. Fifteen of them died. Some starved to death, some froze. Virginia Reed captured the drama in a letter to her cousin back home after she had been rescued:

> O Mary I have not wrote you half of the truble we have had but I hav Wrote you anuf to let you now [know] that you dont now whattruble is but thank the Good god we have all got throw and the onely family that did not eat human flesh. we have left everything but I dont cair for that we have got through. but Dont let this letter dishaten [dishearten] anybody and never take no cutofs.

The Reeds and another family shared a little cabin, which was the very cabin that Moses Shallenberger and his companions had built two years before. Though the Reed children did not eat human flesh, they did have to eat their little pet dog. Virginia Reed described the conditions in a letter:

> There was 15 in the cabin we was in, and half of us had to lay a bed all the time, thare was 10 starved to death there we was hadley abel to walk, we lived on littel cash [the dog] a week and after Mr. Breen would cook his meat we would take the bones and boil them 3 or 4 days.

Before they became stranded, Virginia's father, James Reed, had been banished from the group after killing another company member in a fight, so he had gone ahead to California. When his family failed to appear as expected, he began to organize a relief party, but it took them nearly four months to get through the snowy mountains to the victims. Virginia described her feeling upon laying eyes on the advance party of rescuers, who came ahead of her father's group:

> Oh, my Dear Cousin you don't know how glad I was, we run and met them one of them we knew. . . . They staid thare 3 days to recruet [rest] us a little, so that we could go. Thare was 20 started all of us started and went a piece and Martha and Thomas [the younger Reed children] giv out, and so the men had to take them back. . . . O! Mary, that was the hades [hardest] thing yet to come on and leiv them thar.

Virginia's sister Patty, just eight years old, was a pillar of strength. When the first rescuers came, Patty and her brother Thomas were too weak and too sick to travel. According to Virginia, when the family parted, Patty said, "Well, ma, if you never see me again, do the best you can." Virginia added, "The men said thay could hadly stand it it maid them all cry."

Patty must have been destined to survive that horrific ordeal in what became known as "starvation camp." In late February James Reed arrived with a new rescue party. Mr. Reed struggled up the mountains for his children Patty and Thomas. He found everyone near death. Another rescuer carried Tommy, and Mr. Reed took Patty and staggered out of the cabin toward the valley below, where they had stored some food.

But nature showed no mercy. In a cruel twist of fate, a new blizzard swept in as the rescuers crept down the mountains on snowshoes with the survivors. They found still more misfortune when they finally reached the bottom. Bears had taken their provisions and left them with nothing to eat. Patty was starving, freezing, and barely breathing. They finally got a fire started, and Patty's father warmed her cold body. Then he remembered a teaspoon of breadcrumbs he had saved in the thumb of his mitten and fed those crumbs to Patty. She rallied a little, and it was she who ended up giving the men hope. "God has not brought us so far to let us perish now," she whispered. In the end, all four Reed children as well as their parents lived.

In 1850, when she was sixteen, Virginia married John M. Murphy, who interestingly enough was Moses Shallenberger's fellow guard and traveling companion on the trail in 1844. They settled in California and had nine children. Virginia lived to be eighty-eight.

The Donner family also had their heroine in this disaster. Mrs. Donner's two stepdaughters had been rescued by the first relief expedition, but she, her husband, and her three daughters had been too weak to go. When the second rescue team appeared, Mrs. Donner refused to leave her ill husband, but she bribed two of the men to take her three children out. Eliza Donner, then almost four, remembered this scene:

> Mother, fearing that we children might not survive another storm in camp, begged [the men] to take us with them offering five hundred dollars in coin. . . . We collected a few keepsakes and other light articles. . . . Then lovingly she combed our hair and helped us to dress quickly. . . . "I may never see you again, but God will take care of you," she said. . . . [Later] the men left us sitting on a

blanket upon the snow. . . . We watched them, trembling, lest they leave us there to freeze.

It was six-year-old Frances who provided encouragement. She hugged her sisters, Georgiana and Eliza, as they sat huddled together on the blanket and with grave maturity said, "Don't feel afraid. If they go off and leave us, I can lead you back to mother by our foot tracks on the snow." The men did return, but only to take the girls to another cabin, where the adults were more dead than alive. "There without a parting word they left us," Eliza said. The Donner sisters were finally brought down in the third rescue effort, but both their parents died in the mountaintop morgue. Eliza Donner married Sherman O. Houghton in 1861. She and her sisters all lived long lives in California.

One of the most poignant items on display at the Sutter's Fort museum in Sacramento is a little wooden doll and a lock of her grandmother's hair that Patty Reed brought down from the mountains. It is a touching reminder of what is important to children.

Animals

Prince [his dog] was sitting up on his haunches and crying almost like a child. . . . The sand was as though it had been cooked in the oven. I gathered Prince up in my arms and carried him to our wagon. . . . He had never ridden til this time. "Poor little Prince" we fondly called him.

—Memoir of Charles Frederick True, age sixteen in 1859

From the oxen that pulled the wagons, to the wild game that provided food, to the loyal pet dogs that suffered every step along with their owners, animals played a unique and important role on the Overland Trail. Some animals, such as bears and wolves, were a threat to the pioneers; others, such as oxen, provided vital assistance. Depending on the circumstances, dogs might fall somewhere in between. As with all stories of pioneer life, these accounts of animals on the trail are humorous, heartbreaking, and even heroic. In the end, however, the animals fared worse than the people.

Dogs: Help or Hindrance?

Many emigrant families had to leave their dogs behind because they had room for only the bare essentials on the trip. Others gave up their pets believing that the journey would be too difficult for the animals. Several young pioneers mentioned the anguish they felt at parting with beloved pets. Joseph Fish, age seven in 1846, remembered this sad scene as his ferry pulled out from the Mississippi River shore at Nauvoo:

> My father did not have a team but loaded what few effects that he had into the wagon that he had made. . . . As we slowly left the Illinois shore my sister Anna Marie and I looked back and there we saw our favorite dog Prince standing on the bank, too old to attempt to swim the river. He had been our [long] companion and to leave him thus brought the tears to my eyes.

As the John Scott family rolled away from their home in Illinois bound for Oregon in 1852, their howling family dog raced after the wagons while the children shouted at him to go home. The dog eventually stopped howling, went back to the family home, refused to eat, and died of a broken heart.

For the dogs that did come along, the journey was arduous, and most did not survive the trip. Yet some devoted dog owners could not bear to leave their pets. Charley True ignored his neighbors when they questioned the wisdom of taking his little puppy Prince on the trail in 1859:

> Quite a few suggested that owing to his unusually short bow legs and stocky body, he would be unable to travel such a distance. We would not think of parting with our pet, so along he came, week after week, and month after month.

Prince made it all the way to California, with a lot of help from Charley. But such success stories were rare. Dogs on the trail often starved, drowned, died of exhaustion, were killed by wild animals, or were shot as a nuisance. When food got terribly scarce, some were even eaten by their owners.

When dogs in large companies barked too much or got in the way, it was not uncommon for the trail captains to order them killed. The Mormons were ordered to keep careful watch over their pets, keeping them tied up or in the wagons, or else they would be shot. Such actions were certainly harsh, but the company leaders believed them justified. In addition to being a bother, dogs could become rabid. They were also known to cause cattle stampedes.

One of the most distressing episodes involving dogs on the trail occurred in Dr. Elijah White's 1842 company to Oregon. The party's twenty-two dogs were sniffing, barking, and running in front of the wagons. Near Elm Grove, Kansas, the wagons were halted and there was a strange silence while the men huddled together and whispered. The whispers became shouts, then quiet again. Dr. White recorded what happened next:

> Here, by two-thirds vote, it was determined to kill all the dogs of the company, having been informed that in crossing the mountains . . . these animals were apt to become rabid, as timber was scarce and consequently water [would be scarce] which they so much required in the heat of summer.

Gunshots rang out, bringing the yelping of dying dogs, the screams of children, and the cries of women. According to Dr. White, "This action did not at all accord with the feelings of the ladies."

While dogs were often viewed as a liability on the trail, there were occasions when they became lifesavers. The Reed family's dogs kept the children from freezing one frigid night in 1846. Virginia Reed wrote about it in a letter to relatives:

> We laid down on the ground [and] spred one shawl down, and we laid down on it and spred another over us, and then put the dogs on top. It was the couldes night you most ever saw; the wind blew and if it haden bin for the dogs we would have Frozen.

Two months later the Reeds had to eat their favorite dog, Cash, to keep from starving. Thus Cash saved their lives twice.

Some pioneers reported finding devoted dogs along the trail standing guard over their owners' graves. Seventeen-year-old Granville Stuart, en route to California with his father and brother in 1852, described this poignant episode in his reminiscences:

> Cholera was raging among the emigrants all along the road and many were dying. . . . One evening we camped near five abandoned wagons. Close by were freshly made graves and by one of the wagons was a large yellow dog, with a bushy tail. He was thin and nearly starved. I coaxed him to me and divided my supper [with him]. He then went back and laid down by one of the graves and there remained all night. In the morning I called him, and fed him well.

When the men started to move out, Granville beckoned to the dog. It hesitated. Slowly it moved a few steps, then went back to the grave and began to howl. "Oh! so mournfully," Granville wrote. He continued:

> We stopped to see what he would do. He quit howling and turned and came slowly to us. His pitiful howling was his leave taking of the loved one who lay there in the lonely grave. My eyes filled with tears.

The dog, which Granville named Watch, followed him to California, and it became his faithful companion. During the first few months of 1853, Watch helped keep Granville and his brother from starving:

> My dog Watch . . . was still my constant company. He had a very keen scent and he would track a squirrel and then bark until we [went out] to shoot it.

On his way to the gold mines in 1850, John Steele, eighteen, noted this scene of another incredibly loyal canine near Independence Rock:

Before reaching the river we passed an abandoned wagon. It looked like a splendid outfit . . . and under the wagon lay a faithful watch dog, dying at his post. When we touched any article, he showed his teeth. . . . I doubt whether he was able to stand, but he would not be coaxed, and we [had] not the heart to shoot him, so we left him to his fate.

Other Pioneer Pets

In addition to dogs, young emigrants had a few cats and pet birds. Many had horses or ponies. Sometimes a farm animal, such as a calf or a lamb, was adopted as a pet. The Pratt children, Ellen, Frances, Lois, and Ann, became devoted to a special chicken in 1848. Their mother penned this account when the bird was lost:

[The children] could scarcely be restrained from racing back on foot to recover the lost treasure. [She] was such an extraordinary hen, and had traveled 1000 miles and knew the wagon it belonged to.

Sadly, they could not stop to look for the chicken, but even if they had, it would probably have been fruitless, as the bird had likely been taken by someone or killed by an animal.

Children occasionally made friends with wild squirrels, prairie dogs, and baby buffalo for a while. One youngster even kept a young grey eagle. Seventeen-year-old Eliza Ann McAuley had a most unusual pet:

June 6. While out with the cattle the boys Caught a little antelope and brought it to camp. . . . Our antelope, Jenny, is a great pet in camp and is equally fond of Margaret [her older sister] and me. She bleats and cries if either one is away from her.

Unfortunately, six weeks later Eliza's antelope met an unhappy fate:

July 21. We have met with a sad loss today. Our pet antelope, Jennie, was playing around the camp and the dogs belonging to a large camp of Indians espied her and gave chase. The Indians tried to rescue her, but could not. They then offered to pay us in skins and covers. We told them it was an accident and they were not to blame.

Beasts of Burden

The pioneers owed a lot to the lowly oxen. They were strong and less temperamental than mules or horses and would eat almost anything, so they were the preferred animal to pull wagons. Horses sometimes pulled wagons, but pioneers often just rode them, especially to herd cattle. Mules pulled carts, hauled packs, and carried the occasional passenger. But mules, not considered one of God's nobler beasts, resisted the harness and did not easily learn to obey commands. These animals had a tarnished reputation for stubbornness long before the great western migration ever began.

Any large domestic animal might be yoked up to a wagon. Charley True's company, bound for California in 1859, had a rather odd team. They had a little black ox called Blackie teamed with their cow Starry. The pair got the family to their destination, however, which was more than many a grand horse and carriage accomplished.

Eleven-year-old Lucy Henderson and her family also had an unusual team. By the end of their journey in 1846, nearly all the Hendersons' oxen and horses had either died, gotten lost, or become too weak to pull the wagon. Lucy recollected, "We had six heifers, which father yoked up in place of our lost oxen, and they brought us through to Oregon!"

Horses were perhaps the most highly valued work animals on the trail. Most pioneer children learned to ride a horse at a young age. All five of the Scott sisters rode horseback along part of the trail, allowing them to do a bit more exploring than they could do on foot. Twelve-year-old Elizabeth Keegan of St. Louis was privileged enough to have a horse of her own during her 1852 trip to California. As she wrote to her brother and sister, still back home: "I rode through on horseback and I had a fine opportunity to see and examine everything of note on the way."

Jean Frederick Loba, then eight, remembered a horse his father traded for in 1854:

At Fort Kearney, [Nebraska] which seemed the remote outpost of civilization, my father exchanged a gold watch which was not needed for a very much needed and splendid black horse. He was a fine creature with Arab blood in his veins, and we called him Baal. Strong swift and gentle, he became the pet of all the children, and it was on his back that I first learned the delight of riding a horse.

In 1852 Etty Scott, age eleven, had a horse that was hard to handle:

I was given charge of an old mare, who had one eye. Her name was Shuttleback on account of the shape of her back.... She was a big powerful animal and ... she would kick and plunge and many a time threw me off.... One day we had traveled long in the heat, and needed water. I was about a mile behind the train and off at the side of the road a grove of willows was growing and it looked like water might be there.

Etty and the mare investigated, but they got mired in the mud. Etty yelled for help. After her father rescued her, "I fully expected punishment," she noted, "but my father just picked me up, slapped the mare and said 'now go on.'"

Cow Tales

Emigrants recorded some unusual stories involving cows. Among the hundreds of men heading for gold in 1849 was a young man who "packed through on a cow." One cow with a Mormon company in 1847 got lost during a stampede and traveled back to Winter Quarters, 230 miles away.

Mr. Frederick Piercy, a Mormon pioneer with Daniel Miller's 1853 company, told of a cow with a taste for the exotic. One day Mr. Piercy carefully washed his red silk handkerchief in the Platte River and laid it on the grass to dry. Soon,

> One of the young girls in camp said: 'There's a critter a eaten some-thing.' Sure enough . . . I saw the bright red corners of my best silk handkerchief vanish into a cow's throat. I learned it was no uncommon thing for these animals to appropriate such delicate morsels.

Margaret McNeil, a thirteen-year-old en route to Zion in 1859, seemed to have a special bond with her cow. Margaret took care to find the best grass for the cow, and the animal repaid her in some-times unexpected ways:

> Every morning I would rise early and get our breakfast for the family and milk my cow so that I could hurry and drive her on ahead of the company. I would let her eat in all the grassy places until the company had passed on ahead, then I would hurry and catch up with them. . . . Had it not been for the milk, we would have starved. Being alone most of the time I had to get across the rivers the best I could. Our cow was a Jersey and had a long tail. When it was necessary to cross a river, I would wind the end of the cow's tail around my hand and swim across with her.

Newborn calves presented a dilemma. The little calves could not keep up on the long journey, so unless the emigrants found a way to accommodate them, they often had to be given away or killed. But a cow's maternal instinct would make her wander off in search of her baby. Seventeen-year-old Welborn Beeson wrote in May 1853, "Oceole had a calf tonight. I shot it because it could not travel."

The next day brought an unsurprising development. "Oceole got away and went back. I had to go about 10 miles. Some men had met her and caught her."

Thomas Cropper, age fourteen in 1856, recalled using some grisly but effective trickery on some bovine mothers. "We [killed] the calves and took their skins along. The cow would follow the skin."

Calves were not without value, however, and some pioneers arranged to keep them by such means as slowing down for awhile or putting the calves into the wagons. One company in 1853 had a problem when they had to cross a river with new calves and their milk-engorged mothers. As emigrant author Phoebe Goodell Judson described the scene, one young girl yelled to her father, "Oh, papa, mama says them cows can't swim with their bags full of milk." So the man loaded the calves onto a ferry and started across. When the cows heard their babies start to cry, they plunged into the water. Soon they had all made it safely to the opposite bank.

Walking the Trail on Four Feet

The lack of good water along certain long stretches of the trail was as much a hardship for the animals as for the people. The livestock suffered terribly from thirst in the desert, and when they did find water it was often bad. It was very difficult to keep the animals from drinking the harsh alkali water of the salt flats in Utah and Nevada. Hundreds of them died from consuming this water. Susan Noble, age fifteen, recorded her mostly futile efforts to protect her family's stock in 1847:

> My, how we boys and girls worked day after day to keep our cows and sheep from drinking too large a dose at one time of this brackish water. The weather was so hot, and the animals increased in their thirst by the salty country that, in spite of our poundings and pleadings, they would gorge themself upon the morbific, soapbubbly stuff and then almost immediately became sick.

Lucy Henderson, years after the fact, related how her family made special preparations to sustain their cattle through some arid country in 1846:

There [would be] no water at all, so we filled every keg and dish with water so the cattle should have water as well as ourselves. We had no grain or hay, so Mother baked up a lot of bread to feed them. When we had finally crossed the desert the cattle smelled water, and ran as hard as they could go, our wagon bouncing along and nearly bouncing us out. We could not stop them.

The desert climate created other problems besides thirst. Animals got sore feet from the alkali soil, and many pioneers made leather shoes for them. Both Welborn Beeson and Eliza Ann McAuley mentioned making shoes for their animals.

The driest, saltiest part of the trail to California, Nevada's Forty Mile Desert, was an animal morgue by 1850. One stretch of desert had "one dead creature every twenty feet," according to one account that year, and another emigrant wrote that he could have "stepped from one dead animal to the next." One pioneer noted that "abandoned, prostrate cattle were often run over by emigrant wagons before they died." The stench here was overpowering. Vultures would often swoop down and "peck out the eyes of an animal not yet dead." Fourteen-year-old Sallie Hester, en route to California in 1849, captured this scene in her journal:

The weary journey last night, the mooing of the cattle for water, their exhausted condition, the cry of 'Another ox down,' the stopping of the train to unyoke the poor dying brute, to let him follow at will or stop by the wayside and die, the weary, weary tramp of men and beasts, worn out with heat and famished for water, will never be erased from my memory.

Water could prove nearly as deadly as the lack thereof. Many animals drowned as they tried to ford the raging rivers. The Platte

Missouri River Crossing at Council Bluffs, by William Henry Jackson.
—Courtesy Scotts Bluff National Monument

River swept away a lot of animals one day in 1853, if seventeen-year-old Helen Stewart's report is accurate:

The river was very high it is four miles wide, and sand bottom.
. . . There was a man going to cross the river with a drove of sheep
and he put in thirty thousand and he got out five thousand.

Moses Shallenberger, then seventeen, witnessed a bizarre incident as his company tried to cross the Missouri River near Council Bluffs in 1844:

The wagons crossed in a rude flat-boat, and it was intended to
swim the cattle . . . but some were stuck in the sand, which had
been tramped by them untill it was as tenacious as quicksand.
When the water receded, a few of the mired cattle were dug out

with pick and spade, but others were fastened so securely and deep, they were abandoned.

Some water was infested with leeches, and animals occasionally died from having these parasites on their throats and stomachs. Scalding hot springs could also be hazardous. One emigrant heading east along the California Trail in 1846 saw his dog, ironically named Lucky, rush into the boiling water at Brady's Hot Springs in present Nevada and get scalded to death. Mr. James Clyman wrote this entry soon after it happened:

Poor fellow not knowing that it was Boiling hot he deliberately walked in to the caldron to slake his thirst and cool off his limbs ... and [to] my sorrow he scalded himself to death. I felt more for his loss than any other animals I ever lost in my life as he had been my constant companion in all my wanderings.

At least two other dogs died at the same spot.

The pioneers usually tried to help their animals survive the difficult conditions as best they could. If the cattle got sick from ingesting bad water or food, their owners administered some strange home remedies. Welborn Beeson reveals his company's cure for bovine indigestion:

June 16. We stayed in camp all day as some of the cattle seem sick by having eaten so much last night. We poured melted lard down their throats out of a long necked bottle or cow's horn and it seemed to help them.

Other emigrants used various combinations of lard, salt pork, vinegar, or molasses for their livestock's stomach distress.

Sometimes the only food and water available to the animals on the trail was so bad, they refused to consume it. One pioneer coaxed his horse into taking a drink by making some unappealing water into coffee. Another added salt to the coarse prairie-grass hay to make it more palatable for his oxen.

When one of the cattle in Eliza Ann McAuley's party had an unfriendly encounter with a snake, Eliza noted another veterinary technique:

> Friday, April 30th. One of the steers got snake-bitten on the nose this evening. It swelled very fast and gave the animal much pain, but an application of tobacco and whiskey soon relieved him. That is the only use our party makes of those articles.

When a smaller animal was ill or injured, its owner would sometimes make room in the wagon for it, as Charley True did with "poor little Prince." But in spite of tender loving care, the creatures didn't always make it, as this memory from Rachel Emma Woolley, age twelve in 1848, shows:

> We had an old pig that was expecting babies that day, and she had to ride in the buggy, as father was very anxious to save the little pigs, but they all died in consequence of the rough road.

Some trail experiences could be baffling for animals. For example, at Echo Canyon—just inside the border of Utah—animals became frightened at hearing their own moos, oinks, and barks reverberate against the canyon walls and come back. One pioneer wrote, "The cattle seemed startled in Echo Canyon. They seem to think they are being answered by their own kind."

The Mighty Buffalo

The mysterious bison, more commonly known as the buffalo, was the object of much curiosity and excitement for the pioneers, as most had never seen these animals before. Buffalo roamed the western plains in herds of hundreds, thousands, even tens of thousands. At times the herds would run past the wagon trains at a gallop, often creating a dust storm that practically hid them from

A bison bull.
—Tom Ulrich photo

view. The speed with which they could run amazed many observers. Out on the prairie, the pioneers came to rely on these great beasts, hunting them for meat and using their manure for fuel.

Benjamin Bonney, age seven in 1845, later recalled how the cattle reacted to their wild cousins:

> *Whenever oxen smell buffalo they go crazy. They want to join them. ... It is an odd thing that when oxen smell the fresh trail of the buffalo they stop and paw and bellow as if they smelt fresh blood.*

An extraordinary creature, the American bison has an enormous, shaggy head with horns and a bushy beard. Males can weigh up to two thousand pounds. Though surprisingly fast for its size, the bison does not move gracefully at all, but rather lopes along with its head lowered. Its eyesight is poor, but it has a keen sense of smell and hearing. Herds can be unpredictable, sometimes tolerating the presence of humans, other times stampeding at a small disturbance.

Upon reaching the plains, the emigrants soon learned all about buffalo. John Steele, out looking for some lost cattle, thought he had found their trail but discovered otherwise:

> *Today I learned to distinguish between the track of a buffalo and an ox. At first glance they seem just alike; both have a cloven foot, but the foot of a buffalo is outlined [like] a circle. The ox has a longer foot and the inner toe [is] slightly shorter than the other. Had I known this some days ago, I would not have followed a herd of buffalo, thinking they were oxen.*

Moses Shallenberger observed some fascinating bison behavior in 1844 after shooting a female buffalo (cow): "The entire herd gathered around the wounded cow, sniffing the blood, and pawing and bellowing."

Tragically, millions of bison were slaughtered during the nineteenth century. There was a good market for buffalo skins, used for carriage blankets and other items. In addition, as part of the United States government's campaign to subdue the Indians and claim their land, pioneers were encouraged to kill buffalo, on which the Plains tribes depended for survival. Great bison hunters like Buffalo Bill became heroes. Though Mormon companies and some others did not allow the killing of buffalo for sport, most Americans hunted them frequently. By the turn of the twentieth century, the species had very nearly become extinct.

Stampede!

Buffalo stampedes were awesome and dangerous events. In this account Edward Lenox, then sixteen, remembered how the men in his 1843 company had to direct the galloping herd away from their camp:

> *The pilot played his part... leading a herd of over three thousand bellowing, fighting, buffalo past the men. Seven of them fell dead*

as they passed the ledge of rock where the men were posted, and the great herd went plunging over the precipice twenty feet high, into the great South Platte River, two hundred yards from our wagons, where scores of them were drowned.

Merely sensing the presence of running buffalo could in turn cause cattle to stampede. In fact many things could inspire cattle, which were particularly jumpy in unfamiliar territory, to take off en masse, such as a sudden loud noise or the sight of a wolf or coyote. Most emigrant men and boys had to jump from their beds and chase after cattle at least once during their westward journey. Sixteen-year-old George Bean gave one account in 1847:

When we reached the forks of the Platte River, a stampede occurred. Hearing the uproar, I sprang out and took after the herd, bareheaded and barefooted, [I ran] over and got ahead of the cattle first of all the men, though some were on horseback. We surrounded and got [most] back ... into the corral again. ... We suffered the loss of 46 head of cattle.

Wondrous Wildlife

From the odd antics of the prairie dog to the terrifying midnight howls of the wolf, western wildlife aroused much wonder in the pioneers. Wild horses were among the most magnificent animals, seen by many and captured by a few. One pioneer in 1850 caught and tamed "the most beautiful wild white horse I ever saw," reported Mormon company leader Wilford Woodruff.

Grizzly bears were the most feared of all wild animals, though they were rarely seen. This journal entry by John Steele reveals how strong these bears are:

Following up a ravine about half a mile we found an ox which the bear had not only killed but dragged the whole distance. Here, as he attempted to turn with the burden from the road, it became *entangled among some small trees whereupon he torn one of the hams from the body and carried it away.*

Though not quite as dangerous as grizzlies, wolves were also feared. Their often aggressive behavior gained them no praise in western journals. Though wolves seldom attacked people, their negative image loomed large. Rachel Emma Woolley had a vivid memory of watching these wild canines feast on dead cattle where her company was camped in 1848:

The stench was awful and the wolves were as thick as sheep. It seemed as though they had gathered for miles around. There wasn't a wink of sleep that night for any of us. The wolves were so bold they would come right into camp, and [they] would put their feet on the wagon tongues and sniff in at the end of the wagon.

Wolves are scavengers, so pioneers had to be careful about where and how they buried their loved ones. They are also predators. One small boy who wandered away from camp was attacked and eaten by wolves "who picked his bones clean," according to Mr. Lorenzo Waugh in 1852. This type of episode was rare, however.

Charley True never forgot a scary face-to-face encounter he had with some wolves in 1859:

I froze in fright, all sense of power gone. I was simply terrified at the sight of five immense gray Humboldt wolves which had come from the sagebrush. . . . They crouched motionless. . . . Their eyes! They appeared to be electrified.

Fortunately, as usually happened in these situations, the animals just returned Charley's stare, then walked away.

This 1853 account by Mr. Frederick Piercy captures the fearsome night music of the wolf:

The wolves howled at night most dismally, causing an almost indescribable sensation. They seemed to wail and gnash their teeth for the fun of the thing. It was however, no joke to me to be hushed to sleep with such music.

The pioneers felt that coyotes were no better, as Jean Loba's comment shows:

Many nights as we lay in our tent, or under the wagons, we heard either the loud barking of the gray wolf, or sharp querulous tones of the coyote, snapping and snarling [near] our head.

Not all wild animals were so intimidating. As the big wagons rolled over their underground homes, alarmed prairie dogs barked and scurried around. These funny little creatures darted in and out of their holes with amazing speed. If quick on the trigger, a pioneer might have one for supper. Abigail Scott, seventeen, noted her first close look at this burrowing rodent in 1852:

They killed a prairie dog and brought it to the camp. They are curious looking animals, resembling the rat, squirrel and rabbit, and look as if they might be good eating tho' we do not like to be the first to try them.

Those who braved the taste test pronounced prairie dogs "excellent eating." Another western rodent popular as small game was the jackrabbit. Charley True wrote that he saw "hundreds and hundreds" of them on his trip.

European immigrants on their way out west had some enlightening encounters with animals unknown to them. Jean Loba's father was from Switzerland. In a wagon train headed for Utah, he killed a skunk one day and brought it back to camp. Jean later recalled this amusing episode:

Captain Campbell called upon my father to explain to him the utter impossibility of ever deodorizing this little animal. Although I remember distinctly that my father had it in his mind to skin it, bury the pelt for a few days and thus save its beautiful fur. He was persuaded to throw it away, [and] his entire suit of clothes had to be burned.

—SUMMARY—

Wild and domestic animals were very much a part of the pagentry and pathos of trail life. For domestic animals, the hazards of the trail were even more threatening than they were for humans. One historic researcher estimated that there were eighteen oxen deaths for every human one. Probably about two-thirds or more of the four-footed creatures beginning the trek west either died or were lost, abandoned, sold, or stolen. Of those that died, many were killed by humans for food or other reasons; others drowned, were killed by wild animals, or died from exhaustion, thirst, starvation, toxic water, parasites, disease, or mistreatment.

It is interesting to consider the sacrifice of the animals and their overlooked role in America's western expansion. In their own subtle way, by providing food, labor, protection, and companionship, animals helped the pioneers fulfill their dreams in Oregon, California, Utah, and elsewhere.

CHARLES FREDERICK TRUE

Charley True didn't write his memoirs until the early twentieth century, when he was in his seventies, but his story seems as vivid and fresh as if he had just arrived in California. Charley left Minnesota for the West Coast with his parents, his brother John, and his sisters Mary and Carro in 1859. But his real journey had begun in 1856, when the Trues moved from Maine to Minnesota. Thirteen at the time, Charley later remembered traveling by steamer ship to Ohio:

> *High, turbulant waves and howling winds on the Atlantic [Ocean] . . . gave us our first shaking-up. We clung to one another, not realizing that this was only the first of many adventures which lay ahead for our family. . . . We were soon off with a Lake Erie steamer. . . . Our little steamer with its side wheels rolled and nearly stood on end. . . . It was impossible to move about as our small craft met the oncoming rollers and fierce tempest.*

The family spent a year with Charley's paternal grandfather in Mount Vernon, Ohio. In speaking of Old Tom, one of his grandfather's horses, Charley reveals a hidden history:

> *This horse was not without distinction in his time, as he had for years in the 1840s and 1850s been used for night work in relaying slaves into Canada. Many a night he had worked hauling a heavy load of run-away slaves and their few belongings.*

Charley's family continued to Minnesota by train, then took another steamer up the Mississippi River to the place where they settled, Owatonna, in southern Minnesota. There, they faced colder weather than they had expected, accompanied by raging blizzards. The more Charley's parents heard of the ideal climate of the West, the more unbearable to them became the winters of Minnesota:

> *They pictured it [California] a land divinely clad in vernal splendor, with a never-ending charm of coloring, resting on its imposing mountain peaks, its deep canyons, beautiful mirrored lakes and wide fertile valleys.*

In the spring of 1859 the Trues readied their getaway:

One morning [father] and mother gathered us all together and told us we were going to California. . . . Finally all arrangements had been completed, and we said our goodbyes to our friends as they gathered about our new covered wagon with its strong canvas top painted a bluish gray, making it waterproof. It was May 1st, 1859 that we started, I was then sixteen. Our team did not take kindly to leaving and, in fact, for several days showed disapproval when turned out to feed, by trying to run away and return home. . . .

Our progress was slow, but by keeping at it every day, six days a week, we at last came in sight of Council Bluffs. . . . Here we had our first real pleasure, a ride on an antiquated side-wheel ferry boat [across the Missouri River] loaded with our cows, oxen and wagon. I could just fancy that our patient, fatigued animals . . . were for the ten minutes or so, happy to see everything moving on while they were standing motionless chewing their cuds. . . . [Soon] our oxen and cows heard "gee" and "haw" and tightened their chains in order.

Charley's memories of the westward trek are quoted in various chapters of this book. Upon arriving in California, Charley was surprised to discover what had become of all the men who had rushed there in 1849 expecting to become rich:

We found many deserted log cabins formerly occupied by miners and prospectors. . . . In some instances we found Americans who . . . were still living in cabins they built in 1849 . . . men who had come for gold . . . [but] spent the remainder of their useless lives in idleness . . . rather than return [home] dead broke.

Charley became a schoolteacher, got married, and had a son and daughter. After teaching for several years, Charley was offered a position as a school principal in Alameda, California. Later he moved his family to Hawaii when he got a job as a principal there. By the time the family returned to California, they had another daughter. Charley spent the rest of his life in the Golden State, where he loved walking alone in the woods and hills, meditating on his long journey from coast to coast and beyond.

Adventures and Ordeals

*I shall never forget that winter. . . . We lived on wild tur-
keys and trapped timber wolves, and killed deer. . . . Mother
made fringed shirts and buckskin gloves. She outfitted her
own family with buckskin suits and got good prices for those
she sold.*

—Remembrance of Rhoda Quick, age seven in 1852

To borrow a phrase from author Charles Dickens, the great western migration represented some of the best of times and the worst
of times in American history. The scenery was more spectacular,
the accidents more horrible and bizarre, and the joyful moments
richer than anything the pioneers had experienced before. During
hard times, pioneers had to possess not only courage and strength
but extraordinary resourcefulness. Over the course of their journey they witnessed heroism, treachery, faith, humor, joy, cruelty,
compassion, madness, and much more. This chapter features a
potpourri of trail experiences from the agonizing to the amazing.

Explorations and Discoveries

One sixteen-year-old bride, Sarah Cummins, chose to tangle with
the rugged mountainous route to Oregon in 1845 on foot. While
most pioneers took barges or canoes down the Columbia River,
Sarah stayed with her husband and a few others driving cattle over

the mountains. Sarah's account is unique, for she went where no white woman had gone before, and she did it all while pregnant! How did this petite, eighty-pound expectant mother survive the tramp over tall rocky ridges and down deep ravines of those mountains? Sarah proved that physical limitations have little to do with accomplishments.

Sarah got lost, suffered from frostbitten feet, and subsisted on little more than blueberries. One might think this was a honeymoon from hell, but years later Sarah remembered the beauty, not the hardship:

> My attention was wholly devoted to the majestic hue of Mount Hood as seen from the high Southern slope. . . . Looking upward toward the summit I saw an unusually black looking spot, and after clambering up many hundreds of feet I came upon what seemed to be an extinct crater, and near what seemed to me to be the summit of a mountain. . . . I sat down, lost in thought and admiration of the beautiful and wonderful view that opened before my eyes.

Sarah climbed to 11,240 feet, the highest point in Oregon:

> Seated on eternal snow, looking from over these mountains and hills, across wide valleys into dark glens, above the roar of wind or of water, I was lost in infinity.

It takes an extraordinary optimist to be standing on frozen feet yet look beyond herself to infinity. But seven-year-old Benjamin Bonney did just as well by looking down. By the time the Bonney family got over the Sierra Nevada in the fall of 1845, everyone was exhausted, and the children had blistered, bleeding feet. Little did they know that Benjamin was about to make an amazing discovery:

> At the foot of the Sierras we camped by a beautiful clear ice-cold mountain stream . . . to rest and let the women wash. My sister

Harriet, who was 14, and myself put in three delightful days wading in the stream. On one of the gravel bars I saw what I thought were grains of wheat, but when I picked them up I found they were heavy and of a dull yellow color. I took one of the pieces into camp.

The other children also began to see those pretty rocks. Benjamin handed a jar full of the small golden nuggets to one of the men in the company, a doctor, who whispered to Benjamin's father, "What your boy found today is pure gold. Keep the matter to yourself." But the parents didn't believe the doctor and did not investigate. The doctor died soon afterwards, and no one knows what happened to the jar of nuggets. Gold was not officially discovered until more than two years later, but Benjamin could very well have been the first American to find gold in California! The history books, however, say it was Mr. James Marshall.

Another young pioneer had a date with destiny in 1852. Josephine Smith, an eleven-year-old from St. Louis en route to California with her family, recalled an incident that eventually gave her a place in history. Not far from their camp near the Sierra Nevada the Smiths saw a small cabin in which they found a feverish man, almost dead, according to family lore. It was the famed mountain man Jim Beckwourth. Josephine's mother nursed him back to health. When Beckwourth recovered, he took his kind friends over a new trail through the Sierras, and he asked Josephine to ride with him. "I became the first child to traverse this trail," she later stated.

According to the family, Beckwourth said, "There, little girl . . . there is California! There is your kingdom!" Five years later she boasted to a cousin, "I am now known throughout California as 'the Los Angeles poetess.'" She had just published her first poem at age sixteen. Josephine, who soon after moved to San Francisco and changed her name to Ina Coolbrith, was beginning to gain her "kingdom."

A Spunky Lad

One Mormon urchin from England had quite a few adventures in 1866. Harry (B. H.) Roberts, age nine, had departed in April with his older sister Mary on the *John Bright*. Harry arrived in America with a souvenir: lice! Some teamsters in Council Bluffs noticed the critters in Harry's hair and chopped off his tangled locks with sheep shears.

Harry soon marched off for Utah, but he was totally unprepared, without extra shoes, clothes, or bedding. He must have heard much snickering from the other boys in camp when they saw his "blanket":

The only night covering I had was a petticoat that my sister Mary slipped to me after retiring into the wagon [and] I curled up under the wagon and generally shivered through the night.

B. H. "Harry" Roberts.
—Courtesy LDS Historical Department Archives

This was not the last time Harry would be laughed at. One night after picking up his quota of buffalo chips, Harry, who had been barefoot for several weeks, sneaked into the provisions wagon—where he was not supposed to be. Harry was tired of shivering all night, and the wagon was so warm. Inside he saw a huge barrel and slipped down in it to sleep. He described what happened next in his autobiography:

> To my surprise, I discovered when I let myself down in the barrel that my feet went into about three or four inches of a sticky liquid . . . which turned out to be molasses. The smarting of my chapped feet almost made me scream with pain, but I stifled it. Too tired to attempt to climb out, I remained. . . . It was daylight when I woke up [and] as I crawled out I was greeted by some of the teamsters with yells and laughter. I crept away to scrape off the syrup for there was no change of clothing for me.

Harry walked on, coatless and shoeless, with the temperature dropping more each day. His feet bled and he was freezing at night, but he kept his eyes open for opportunities. On August 20, Harry arrived at Deer Creek, Wyoming, and saw the smoldering ruins of several log cabins. Indians had attacked and killed some settlers, and, against the captain's orders, Harry decided to investgate. His sharp eyes immediately focused on something in a burned cabin—boots! Almost new boots, on a dead man.

Harry looked at his sore bare feet and back at the boots:

> My feet by dint of water, sand, and sun heat had now become black and hard and cracked, through which cracks sometimes the blood oozed.

The boots were way too big, but Harry needed them, so he ran in, grabbed the dead man's feet, and tugged on the boots until they slipped off into his trembling hands. He hid the boots in the provisions wagon at first, but they were on his feet when he marched into Salt Lake a month later.

In the Line of Fire

By 1862 the Civil War was raging in the states, but traffic on the trail had not ceased. Most emigrant companies were stopped and searched for deserters. Some pioneers had firsthand experiences with Yankee and Rebel soldiers. William Henry Freshwater, age eleven, left from England by ship, then by train from New York City in 1863. He had a scary experience in Missouri and wrote about it in his diary:

> Just before we arrived in St. Joseph, Missouri, the rebels, or bushwhackers, fired two cannonballs through our train. One shot went through the passenger car . . . destroying a great amount of baggage. We stayed in St. Joseph three or four days, afraid to go on because of the rebel soldiers being all through the country. I can truly say I saw a little of the War between the North and the South.

Shipwrecked

Not all pioneers traveled overland to the western American frontier. Some traveled by boat to the West Coast from Australia, China, the Philippines, and other Eastern Hemisphere countries. The Anderson family, which included eight children, was en route from Australia to San Francisco on the *Julia Ann* in 1855. The ship got blown off course on October 4 and crashed into a reef on one of the Scilly Islands.

The passengers were awakened about midnight with the impact, and panicked confusion followed as water rushed into the rooms. People clung to ropes and the deck rail trying to hold on. The pounding of the waves soon smashed the vessel apart. Agnes and Alexander Anderson, seventeen and fourteen, were among several young people who barely escaped with their lives. The passengers used a long rope to climb onto the reef. One passenger described the wreck:

> The hauling line had parted, the forward part of the ship had broken up, and no hope remained for those who were yet clinging

to the quarter deck, but above the roar of the breakers and shrieks of despair, a mother's voice was heard crying, "Agnes, Agnes, come to me." Agnes was seated on the wreck of the main mast, that had floated upon the reef . . . but she sprang to her feet, threw her arms up shrieking, "mother, mother, I come, I come," and plunged headlong into the sea. A sailor . . . seized her by the clothes and drew her back again.

The Andersons survived except for ten-year-old Marion. Four other passengers were lost as well. The fifty-one survivors were able to salvage some food and other essentials from the wreckage. They discovered an island nearby where they built huts and put up tents. The search for fresh water ended when a group of young children discovered some water holes. In addition to fish, the castaways found other things to eat on the island:

They soon discovered that the turtles came up on the beach at night to lay eggs in the sand. The boys in the party were assigned to go out at night and lay [the turtles] on their backs, and the next morning one would be brought in for food. . . . The women improvised their own brand of pancakes by grating the coconut meat and then mixing it with turtle eggs and a little flour. Sharks were caught intermittently and added a little variety to the castaways' diet.

In many ways their situation was pleasant. They could swim in the lagoon and admire the beauty of the island. The children were quite content, but the adults were deeply worried that they would not be rescued. Soon the captain built a crude canoe and with a dozen other men rowed several hundred miles to Bora Bora Island to summon help. The castaways were rescued by the *Emma Packer* on December 2 and taken to Tahiti. The Anderson family reached San Francisco on June 27, 1856—nine months after leaving Australia.

Lost on the Trail

In 1846 the Oregon-bound William Smith family from Iowa took the then untried Applegate Cutoff in an attempt to shorten their difficult journey. Like many others who strayed from the established trails, they met only with more misfortune. Mrs. Ellen Smith wrote:

> Sickness entered the camp and worst of all they lost their way. . . .
> There was nothing to do but to strugel [on, the men] getting so
> Hart Sick and disscouraged they said there was no use in trying,
> they never could get throw that canyon.

Illness and fatigue hindered their progress. Mr. Smith, the captain of the company, tried to cheer them on, but he died suddenly from a heart attack at Cow Crick Canyon in southern Oregon, not far from their destination. By then Louisa Smith, age sixteen, had contracted Rocky Mountain fever. Sensing that death was near, Louisa begged her mother to bury her six feet deep and "pile large rocks on top" of the grave. Louisa had seen what animals did to shallow graves and "did not want wolves to dig her up and eat her."

Mrs. Smith promised her daughter a deep grave, and when Louisa died her mother "selected a prity little Hill" on which to bury her. When the cold, hungry, weary men of the company had dug the grave to four feet, they announced it was deep enough, but Mrs. Smith jumped into the hole and started to dig herself. The men, touched by her devotion, dug two more feet. Mrs. Smith and her surviving children arrived in Oregon in December and took up their land claim.

A Hard Winter

That same year in another company, Ellen and Aurelia Spencer, fourteen and twelve, were left in charge of four younger siblings in Winter Quarters, Nebraska. Their mother had died on the trail in March, and their father was called to England on a church mission in October. The Spencer children barely survived the terrible winters of 1846–47 and 1847–48. Aurelia wrote later:

*While at the Bluffs [Father] was notified to be in readiness . . .
[and] he put up a log cabin into which we moved before it
was finished there being no floor nor door. The winter having
been uncommon in its severity, our horse and all our cows but
one had died, therefore we had no milk nor butter. We really
suffered . . . having nothing but corn-meal, which was stirred
up with water and baked on a griddle. Many a night I have
gone to bed without supper having to wait until I was hungry
enough to eat our poor fare.*

The children all survived their two years in Nebraska and continued to Salt Lake in 1848.

Snowbound

Heber McBride was a thirteen-year-old in the snowbound Martin Handcart Company in 1856. A few days after they had discarded many of their belongings at Deer Creek, Wyoming, to lighten their loads, it turned very cold. They came to the last crossing of the Platte River, and the struggle to get across the ice-clogged, turbulent water weakened the already exhausted Saints. Then it began to snow and sleet. "The crossing of the North Platte was fraught with more fatalities than any other incident," Josiah Rogerson, then fifteen, stated later. They made camp to wait out the blizzard and bury the dead. It was so cold at night that many more died or got sick.

One night was especially bitter, and they wished for the blankets they had thrown out. That night Heber heard his father, who had been designated camp song leader, sing a haunting refrain around a flickering campfire before he went to bed. The next morning Heber went looking for his father:

*While my sister was preparing . . . our breakfast, I went to look for
Father and at last I found him under a wagon with snow all over
him and he was stiff and dead. I felt as though my heart would*

burst. I sat down beside him in the snow and took hold of one of his hands and cried oh, Father, Father. There we was away out on the Plains with hardly anything to eat and Father dead and mother sick and a widow with 5 small children and not hardly able to live from one day to another. . . . I went back to the tent and told Mother. Now to try and write to tell the feelings of Mother and the other children is out of the question.

Soon the company heard that there were supply wagons waiting for them at Devil's Gate. Everyone rejoiced. The next day, they picked up their handcarts with new enthusiasm, but the flesh did not match the spirit. Each step took painstaking effort as they struggled to push the carts forward, slipping and sliding in the snow. Near Independence Rock they met some men with wagons containing some supplies but not much food. Before they could get to the camp at Devil's Gate, they had to cross the swift and frigid waters of the Sweetwater River. "Women shrank back and men wept," read one account. Some of the young men jumped in and helped the others across.

They waited several days at the Devil's Gate camp before more relief came. They became desperate for food. Heber McBride wrote in his autobiography:

My 2 little Brothers would get the sack that had flour in it and turn it wrong side out and suck and lick the flour dust.

Nine-year-old Mary Ellen Normington watched her father grow weaker. One freezing night, he died. Mary Ellen recorded her sorrow:

On November 6, the thermometer registered eleven below zero. [Mother] reached across her sleeping husband to pull a blanket over him. His arm felt stiff and rigid. . . . They wrapped him in a blanket and placed him with thirteen others.

Sisters Ellen and Maggie Pucell, ten and fourteen, suffered terrible frostbite at the camp. Their parents had died on the trail, so they had no one to look after them. Rescuers finally arrived. One of them, Mr. Ephraim Hanks, brought buffalo meat and castile soap:

> Many of the immigrants whose extremities were frozen, lost their limbs, either whole or in part. Many such I washed with water and castile soap until the frozen parts would fall off, after which I would [cut] the shreds of flesh from the remaining portions of the limbs with my scissors.

Ellen sustained the most damage, and her legs had to be amputated just below the knees after she arrived in the Salt Lake Valley. The surgery was performed with a crude hacksaw and no pain medication.

Another handcart group, led by James Willie, had also gotten caught in the same blizzard, just ahead of the Martin company. Mary Hurren, about ten at the time, remembered the agony of cold and hunger in that camp:

> Our small allowance of flour was cooked as a gruel and eaten. . . . Pieces of rawhide on the handcarts were cooked to secure what food value there was. One morning father went out, and with a stick uncovered from the snow a piece of rawhide about a foot square. After washing it, he cut it into small strips and boiled it. Those pieces were given to us to eat. We . . . chewed them as we would gum. . . . The snow was about eighteen inches deep and it was bitter cold. My shoes were worn out, and my feet and legs were badly frozen.

Mary survived. Though Heber McBride lost his father, the five children and their mother lived. Mary Ellen Normington and her sister also made it, as did their mother, though she was near death for several days. In all, over two hundred of the one thousand Saints in the two companies died from starvation, exhaustion, and exposure.

Ellen Pucell, the girl who lost her legs, later married a man named Unthank and had six children. She never allowed her handicap to hinder her from leading a full life and serving others. Her story was seen as heroic enough to warrant a memorial—in 1991, Mormon president Gordon B. Hinckley dedicated a plaque in her memory in Cedar City, Utah.

—SUMMARY—

The journey west was full of adventure as well as tragedy. On the trail, most anything could happen at any time, and the pioneers had to be prepared to meet whatever challenges came up. Survival demanded courage, resourcefulness, and tenacity. In withstanding the incredible hardships they faced, the sturdy youngsters featured here proved themselves to be true heroes. One might conclude that the emigrants' greatest legacy was their remarkable children.

Profile of
THE SAGER CHILDREN

One of the most tragic sagas in trail history was the fate of the seven Sager children. These children were orphaned en route to Oregon in 1844 when their parents died of Rocky Mountain fever about one month apart. Catherine Sager, age ten, was the eldest girl; her two older brothers, John and Francis, were fourteen and twelve. Catherine captured the trauma of this all-too-common tragedy:

> Thus in twenty-six days both our parents were laid in the grave, and we were orphans, the oldest fourteen years old and the youngest five months old.

After Mr. and Mrs. Sager's death, the captain of the company, Mr. William Shaw, and his wife helped look after the orphans, as did the kindly Dr. Theophilos Dagon, who drove the children's wagon for them. Captain Shaw made arrangements for the children to stay with Dr. Marcus and Narcissa Whitman at the famous Whitman Mission near present-day Walla Walla, Washington. When they arrived at the mission in the fall of 1844, it was a scene to melt the coldest heart:

> We drove up and halted. . . . Foremost stood the little cart with the tired oxen lying near. Sitting in the front end of the cart was John weeping bitterly. On the opposite side stood Francis sobbing aloud. On the near side the little girls stood huddled together, bareheaded and bare footed, looking first at the boys and then at the house, dreading we knew not what. . . . Thus Mrs. Whitman found us.

The children soon adjusted to life with the Whitmans, who were strict but caring, but little did they know their ordeal had barely begun. The Whitmans had come west to teach the native peoples about their faith (Presbyterian). They had been working with the local Cayuse people for some years when a severe epidemic of measles broke out, and because they had no resistance to the disease, many of the Indians died. The Cayuse could not understand why the white settlers recovered and they did not. They thought a curse had been put on them, and they blamed Dr. Whitman.

On November 29, 1847, a band of Cayuse attacked the mission and killed the Whitmans and twelve others, including John and Francis Sager. The Indians took the survivors—more than fifty women and children, among them the Sager girls—as captives. A few days after the tragedy, one of the sisters, five-year-old Hannah Louise, died from measles. Several weeks later, famous trader Peter Skene Ogden negotiated the release of the prisoners, trading merchandise for their freedom.

The surviving Sager children were taken in by separate families in Oregon. Catherine, now thirteen, found a stable home, but her sisters were not so lucky. Elizabeth and Henrietta, ten and three in 1848, were shuffled from family to family, and Matilda Jane may have gotten the worst deal of all, for her foster home was abusive. Matilda, who was eight when she was placed with a minister and his wife, suffered great physical and emotional pain with this family:

> Once [her foster father] was going away on a trip. He told me to go and cut a thick switch. I thought he wanted it for his horse. . . . I brought the switch. He called to me and seizing me by the shoulder, gave me an unmerciful beating. I asked, "What have I done?" He said, "Nothing. . . . I am going away. The chances are you will do something to deserve a beating while I am gone, and I won't be here to give it to you."

Matilda was eighty-two when she told her story. She recalled another traumatic incident, when the minister brought her to a public hanging:

> Presently they brought out a man and hanged him. I was horrified. He [her foster father] said, "I brought you to see the hanging to impress on your mind what happens to people who do not mind their elders and do exactly what they are told." It took me months to forget the horrible sight.

Matilda ran away and married a thirty-one-year-old miner when she was fifteen to escape the torment, but her marriage was not happy. Catherine Sager wed Clark Pringle at age sixteen, and they settled near Salem, Oregon. When she married, Catherine sent for Elizabeth and Henrietta, who lived with Catherine and her husband until they themselves married. Henrietta moved to California, where she was accidently killed by a bullet aimed at her husband. The three surviving Sager sisters lived out their lives in relative peace, yet the painful memories of past tragedies remained with them for the rest of their lives.

EPILOGUE
Life in "Paradise"

There were funds set apart for the poor and the Church would have provided for us a meager subsistence for people were not allowed to starve; but [Mother] could not think of living on charity. . . . It was a time of great trials.

—Autobiography of Mary Jane Mount, age fourteen in 1852

The hardships of the journey west prepared the young people well for life on the frontier, for most discovered with Mary Jane Mount that "it was a time of great trials," and often the "elephant" was worse at the end of the trail. Fortunately, the young people learned the importance of hard work and perseverance during the long journey.

Even the more affluent emigrants had their hardships in getting established in the new territory. The new homesteads were generally nothing more than a plot of bare, uncultivated land. There was much to be done in building a home and preparing the grounds for farming or ranching. Edward Lenox, sixteen, did his share when he got to Oregon in 1843: "The fields were not fenced at all, and so father and I went to work at once, making rails and fencing in the fields."

Mary Jane and other young emigrants eventually did find happiness and prosperity in their new home. Despite her ordeal at "starvation camp" in the winter of 1846–47, at thirteen Virginia Reed could write to her cousin about her contented life in California a year later:

> We are all very well pleased with Callifornia particularly with the climate. . . . It is a beautiful Country it is mostley in vallies it aut [ought] to be a beautiful Country to pay us for our trubel getting there. . . . We are all verry fleshy. I weigh 80.

Is This Paradise?

Conditions in the Valley of the Great Salt Lake were among the worst. In 1847 there were only a few log cabins, "a few sunflowers," and a high adobe wall when Ann Cannon, George Bean, and the others arrived in their Zion. There was no way to obtain food except to bring it in by wagon. Nearly two thousand Mormons shared the bleak country by the end of October, and they had a lot to do and a lot to learn that first winter. Ann Cannon, age fifteen, endured mud and meager rations:

> We had been told that no rain fell in the valley, and so they had covered the roofs with plain board and then with clay. . . . One morning Aunt went next door and found a sister in bed with an umbrella over her, and the black mud streaming down around her in bed. We went to bed and Uncle and Aunt sat in front of the fire with a big canvas umbrella over them.

Yet the Saints stuck it out. "We had lots of trials but the Lord made the back equal to the burden," Ann wrote later.

Edwin Pettit, then fourteen, also remembered the mud in Salt Lake that year:

> Many a time we have stood with an umbrella over the table to keep the water from coming through on our food, and tin pans set over the bed to catch the water that dripped through the mud roof.

Mary Jane Mount, fourteen, spent a lonely snowbound winter in the Wasatch Mountains soon after she arrived in the valley in 1852. It was a time filled with much despair and little sunshine:

Our miserable shanty being dark and cold we were glad to keep large fires, logs being put on sometimes which it took two men to lift. We had our yule log for Christmas, but were scant of good cheer. The wind whirled over the mountains, and came down the chimney, often filling the room with smoke and ashes. . . . We often found snow nearly to the top of the door and had to dig a way out.

Mary grew so desperate for new clothes that her mother made some dresses from the tent and wagon covers they had used to cross the plains. "No city belle was ever prouder of her fine array than I was of my new dress," she wrote. Mary was quite studious and wrote poetry, which she dreamed of someday getting published.

In Oregon, the Quick family was another that had some rough early years. Seven-year-old Rhoda Quick and her four siblings reached Oregon in good health in 1852, but Rhoda later recalled the bleak years that followed:

We couldn't bring much in the way of equipment . . . so we lived off the country. The settlers made homemade furniture and the women cooked in fireplaces. We children went barefoot the year round. When I used to turn out early on frosty winter mornings to do the milking and other chores my feet would get so cold I would make the cows that were lying down get up so I could stand on the ground where they had been lying to warm my feet. The first winter we were here we lived on milk and butter, deer meat and other game, for we didn't have a dust of flour in our cabin.

J. D. Matlock was fourteen when his family crossed the plains. They settled near present Eugene, Oregon. It was there that J. D. first went to school, first wore shoes, and first got "whaled" by a schoolteacher:

The first time I was ever in a school house was at the school at Goshen. I was 15 years old. . . . I had gone barefoot all my life, but Mother made me put on shoes to go to school. The teacher told us not to take our shoes off at noon for fear we might catch cold. I got the whole bunch to shed their shoes and go barefoot, for how could you run fast with shoes on?

Of course J. D. got in trouble. When he began to talk back, the teacher "whaled me till he was nearly worn out."

The American Dream Was Hard Work

Elisha Brooks was not yet twelve when he got to California, and it took him a long time to save up some money. Fortunately the trail had prepared him for an arduous life. Soon after he arrived he began working near the mines:

Rising at three o'clock in the morning in summer and four in winter, seven days a week for four years . . . [I] delivered milk on foot through a straggling mine town. . . . After herding stock all day, the trip to town was repeated in the evening. . . . [The] milk was carried on horseback in cans slung in canvas bags.

It was through hard work like this that the emigrants made their farms and businesses successful in the new country. This recollection of Andrew J. Masters illustrates the point:

My parents [came] to the Willamette Valley [in 1843]. . . . In 1856, I was the oldest boy and had to do the plowing with two yoke of oxen and attend to the farm work. I was 11 years old. . . . . When I was a boy all I knew was to work from sunrise to sunset and mind my parents. It never occurred to me not to obey them. In those days the parents, not the children, were the heads of the family.

Getting an education, too, required hard work and discipline. Catherine Thomas, later Catherine Morris, remembered the work soon after she arrived in Oregon. Catherine was eighty-eight when she shared these memories in 1928:

For my 13th birthday I was given a spinning wheel. This was in 1854. People used to bring in their wool, and we washed, carded, spun and wove it for shares, so we soon had plenty of clothes. Mother used alder bark to dye the cloth brown and oak bark to dye it butternut color. . . . [The schoolteacher] charged $10 a term for each pupil. . . . Some of the young men were 20 years old and the girls 16 or 17. I think they did as much sparking [courting] as studying. [The teacher] kept a bunch of heavy hazel switches in the corners of the schoolhouse, so wherever he was he could get one right away, and he sure knew how to use it. . . . Because we were so busy with our work we appreciated all the more the occasional social gatherings and parties we went to.

Meet Some of the Young Pioneers a Few Years Later

It took eleven-year-old Lucy Henderson's family nearly eight months to reach Oregon. Their journey had been filled with hardship and hunger, which continued when they reached the end of their journey:

We [arrived] December 17, 1846, and father did not get there until Christmas Day. After a week or so we moved into a cabin, there was no floor in the cabin, just earth. There was but one room [and] a big chest and Mother filled this full of clothing, and Betty [a sister] and I slept in that. We lived on boiled peas and boiled wheat that winter.

Lucy Henderson (Deady). —Courtesy Southern Oregon Historical Society

Later, Lucy's father went to California to find gold, and he came back successful. Lucy was then able to attend school in Oregon City. There she met Matthew Deady, a young lawyer. They married when Lucy was seventeen. The bride was very proud of her gown:

My wedding dress was made of bishop lawn and was very pretty. Kate [a school chum] and I made it. The waist was pointed in front and fastened in the back. It had a Dutch neck and was trimmed with . . . silk ribbons. I did not wear a veil, but I wore a white ribbon in my hair. I had white kid slippers and white kid gloves. My bonnet was of straw and was lined with white silk and had broad streamers.

Matthew later became a district judge and then a member of the House of Representatives of Oregon Territory. Lucy lived a long life of modest wealth and good health.

The romances of some of the other young pioneers did not fare as well. Several young men were smitten with vivacious Rachel Emma Woolley during her youth. Emma (she used her middle name) had chosen a suitor, while her mother had chosen another. Emma learned that her beau, however, was playing the field and she was crushed. "Many a time I cried nearly all night," Emma admitted. Since her heart was broken and "I did not want to disobey Mother," Emma finally said yes to Joseph Simmons, her mother's choice. "We were married on 18th of December 1851. I had as nice a wedding as could be had in those days." Emma was fifteen.

Joseph was very handsome and became an actor. But he got into debt, then he became ill and died, leaving Emma a widow with ten children at age thirty-five. Nearly destitute, Emma became a midwife to support herself and her children.

Like so many other young Saints, Ruth May, thirteen, had to work hard when she arrived in Utah in 1867. She and her sister Clara attended school for only six months, then took jobs in a factory, "as the family's aim was to buy a home as soon as possible." When the May family later moved to Ogden, Utah, Ruth's father opened his own weaving factory, where Ruth worked as his assistant. "I reeled yarn and wove cloth and finally undertook a man's job running the jack, a machine for spinning scores of threads at a time." With her weaving skills, Ruth made a beautiful wedding outfit in 1873 when she was nineteen and married Jesse Fox. Ruth also became a high official in women's organizations in Utah. She composed music, and some of her songs are still sung today at Mormon meetings.

Etty Scott, who traveled to Oregon in 1852 with her large family, later became a spiritualist and a medium and lived to age eighty-nine. Etty's brother Harvey became a newspaper editor in Oregon and had a long, distinguished career. His views often clashed with those of his feminist sister, Abigail. Another sister, Margaret, died young and Abigail raised one of her children.

After two years in Utah, Edwin Pettit helped herd cattle to California in 1849, when he was sixteen. Soon he had saved enough money to buy two lots in San Bernardino:

Fields were plowed and planted and the town was surveyed of lots of one acre each. I put in a crop of grain and went to farming. I paid $125.00 for a one-acre lot and in a short time bought the next one to it, and paid $200.00 which made me the possessor of a quarter of a block.

After Edwin made this wise real estate investment, he settled down, married a young woman named Rebecca Hood Hill, had a large family, and prospered. He lived to be seventy-eight.

George W. Bean, who went west in 1847 at age sixteen, kept some "notes and jottings" on his trip that he later turned into a journal:

I purchased a small paste-board covered book for a Diary, or journal and copied several pages from smaller books and notes, some incidents and family records. . . . Later, about thirty pages were cut out.

George acquired a little fame during his life. Although he got his left hand shot off by a cannon in 1849, he helped in the building of Zion. George became one of Brigham Young's trusted Indian agents in 1854: "We fulfilled President Young's request to keep Chief Walker peaceable that year of 1854," George wrote. He became a U.S. marshall, then a probate judge, and he held other offices during his lifetime.

The poor spelling in Helen M. Stewart's diary showed her lack of education. Helen yearned for a way to increase her knowledge, so in 1860, when her oldest daughter, Jannet, started school, Helen went with her to study alongside the children. Very few young people were well educated in those days. Unfortunately, Helen died in 1873, at age thirty-eight, leaving seven children.

William M. Colvig, a six-year-old boy on the trail in 1851, later went back to Illinois to study law in the early 1870s:

I went to Tremont, Tazewell County, Illinois and entered Tremont Collegiate Institute. . . . Abraham Lincoln had frequently tried cases at Tremont. The janitor hunted me up a table to use and pointed to the initials "A. L." cut into the table, saying, as he did so: "The man that cut those initials used to be a country lawyer and became President of the United States." I used Abraham Lincoln's old table for the 18 months that I was at school there.

Honest Abe must have inspired William, for he later became a district attorney in Oregon and then was appointed judge.

In 1852 eleven-year-old Elisha Brooks and his family reached their promised land in California, thanks in large part to his contributions. Elisha spent his teenage years as a student in San Francisco, then he became a high school teacher and later a principal. The school he ran excelled in scholastics and discipline. One of his students remarked, "Of all my teachers . . . [the] one that stands out above all others, that had the most impelling influence over my life was Mr. Elisha Brooks."

Elisha married, had a family, and moved to Ben Lomond, California, in 1904. There he built a home, planted an orchard, and became a respected citizen known as the apple king. In 1921 the town of Ben Lomond honored Elisha, then eighty, for his service "in the uplift and advancement of our community."

Growing Families

Most families were large in the nineteenth century, and most of our young pioneers had many children. Edwin Pettit and his wife, for instance, had fourteen children. Ruth May Fox and Margaret Gay Judd Clawson each had thirteen, and Aurelia Spencer Rogers had a dozen children. Virginia Reed Murphy had nine, and Catherine Sager Pringle was a mother eight times. Eliza Ann McAuley Egbert was the mother of seven, while Abigail Scott Duniway stopped at six. Lucy Henderson Deady had just four, and Lizzy Flake Rowan had a small family of three children.

The Midas Touch

A few of our young pioneers achieved great wealth in the West. While it was often hard work and wise investments that brought them prosperity, sometimes they found their fortune in gold. Perhaps the young people who went from rags to riches with the greatest of ease were Sarah and Catherine Rhoads. The Rhoadses arrived in California in October 1846 and settled in the Cosumnes Valley. Sarah, age sixteen, married William Daylor on March 4, 1847, and Catherine, fifteen, tied the knot a few days later with Jared Sheldon. The two men were partners, and both had large ranches, but rich gold claims soon made them two of the wealthiest men in the valley.

As soon as the partners began prospecting, the gold virtually fell into their hands. Local newspapers reported the story of the fabulous finds: "The ravines were so rich that at the end of the week... each one had seventeen thousand dollars." Another report said "the gold was picked out with knives." Not to be outdone by their husbands, the sisters hunted gold around their ranches. They discovered nuggets in their yards and under clumps of grass. The two families went from modest circumstances to great wealth in a few months.

Unfortunately, William Daylor died from cholera in October 1850, and miners killed Jared Sheldon in a claim dispute in July 1851. The wealthy widows did not remain single very long, however. Today there are numerous Rhoads descendants in the greater Sacramento area.

The Los Angeles Poetess

Josephine Smith, age eleven on the trail in 1852, became a well-known poet in California using the pen name Ina Coolbrith. By 1857 she had already published her poetry, while living in Los Angeles. She revealed her opinion of that city in a letter to a cousin:

This is an awful—awful town, Joseph, to live, an awful town. I dont believe there is another place in the world, so small as this town is, that has more crimes committed in it every day.

Ina had a brief, abusive marriage, and one baby who died in infancy. Then she and her mother moved to the Bay Area, where

Ina Coolbrith.
—Courtesy Oakland
Public Library

Ina continued to write poetry, later becoming the first woman member of the elite San Francisco Bohemian Club. In 1919 she was named "Loved Laurel-Crowned Poet of California." Though she had achieved national fame before her death in 1928, she was buried in an unmarked grave next to her mother in the Mountain View Cemetery in Oakland.

Ina's poetry was simple, often dealing with patriotic or religious themes and nature:

CALIFORNIA

Upon my fresh green sods
No king has walked to curse and desolate;
But in the valleys freedom sits and sings,
And on the heights above;

Upon her boughs the leaves of olive boughs,
And in her arms a dove;
And the great hills are pure, undesecrate,
White with their snows untrod,
And mightily with the presence of their God!

An Outstanding Mormon Scholar

Harry Roberts was a London urchin who went on to achieve fame in the Mormon Church. Even though Harry considered his "childhood a nightmare, my boyhood a tragedy," he tried to secure a respectable life by getting an education. It did not happen immediately, however. After an adventuresome journey from England to Salt Lake, Harry spent his early teens in the Utah mines during the 1870s. It was tough work, but it paid well. Miners could be rowdy companions, though, and Harry soon gained a bad reputation with his drinking and gambling. Mormon officials took away his church membership. He appealed his case, though, and the church restored his fellowship. Turning over a new leaf, Harry packed up his one good suit and left for the local university.

Eventually this unruly boy became known as B. H. Roberts, one of the greatest orators in Mormon history, as well as a prolific writer and prominent theologian. He was also elected to a seat in the U.S. Congress, and he was voted "the outstanding scholar in the Mormon Church." He certainly came a long way in his lifetime.

Dedicated to Children

As she had done in Winter Quarters, Aurelia Spencer helped care for and support her siblings during the winter of 1848–49 in the Salt Lake Valley. Aurelia was well educated, for her father believed girls should learn more than stitching clothes and baking bread. In 1851, when she was seventeen, Aurelia married Thomas Rogers. Thomas had been a teamster in the company Aurelia traveled with in 1848. They became acquainted and started to date in Utah. Aurelia looked forward to marriage:

A new life was opening up before me. I was just merging from girlhood into womanhood, being in my seventeenth year. I little realized the care and responsibility of looking after a home of my own. We moved into a log home with two rooms.

Unlike many Mormons of the day, Thomas never practiced polygamy. Aurelia's sisters were plural wives, however. (The church outlawed polygamy in 1890.) While Aurelia and Thomas struggled in poverty for many years, sisters Ellen and Catherine were well off financially. Aurelia helped support her twelve children by sewing and teaching school.

Aurelia became well known in Utah for her concern for children. In 1878 she organized the Primary Association, for children "who should be taught to be better helpers in the home, to improve their manners, [and] to learn everything that is good." The Mormon Church still sponsors this organization. Aurelia was also involved in the women's suffrage movement.

Utah's First Woman Doctor

Romania Bunnell, on the trail in 1855 at age fifteen, would later have an outstanding career in medicine. As a young girl she had attended a female seminary in Indiana, where she studied German, music, and painting. In Utah Romania became a teacher and took care of her three younger siblings when her mother went east in 1857 to claim an inheritance. Mrs. Bunnell returned with a piano, a highly prized possession.

As an adult, Romania went to New York City to study medicine, and she was noted for her long hours in pursuit of excellence:

During the summer vacation while [the other students] were recreating, sea bathing and visiting with friends, I daily plodded studiously up the rugged hill of knowledge, reciting as a private student every day to the professor of physiology. . . . By special permission I joined a class taught by Prof. H. D. Noyes in Bellevue

College. Dr Wm Little said I was the first woman ever admitted to
Bellevue.

In 1873 she became first woman doctor from Utah, specializing in the diseases of the eye and ear in New York City. She was one of the earliest physicians of either sex to specialize. Romania performed over four hundred operations during her career.

Long Lives and Vivid Memories

A few of our young pioneers died young, such as Helen Stewart and Mary Jane Mount, who realized her dream of publishing some poetry before her death in 1890 at age fifty-three. But most lived long and healthy lives. John Steele went back to the Midwest, became a well-known writer and minister, and died at seventy-three. B. H. Roberts was seventy-six when he died. Edwin Pettit and Rachel Emma Woolley were both seventy-eight. Heber McBride lived to be eighty-two, and Aurelia Spencer died in 1922, at age eighty-seven.

Some young pioneers lived even longer. Ann Cannon died at ninety, and Dr. Romania Bunnell Penrose succumbed at ninety-three. Robert Sweeten, who was our youngest teamster at age six, died in 1936 at age ninety-six. Ruth May Fox and Mary Field lived to be over one hundred.

Dozens of the young pioneers were in their eighties and nineties when they recalled their trail days. Amanda Gardener Johnson, a young black pioneer in 1853, was almost ninety when she talked to historian Fred Lockley in the 1920s, as was Barnet Simpson. John McWilliams was eighty-seven in 1919 when he signed a copy of his recollections to a former girlfriend. Elisha Brooks wrote his memoirs when he was eighty-one, seventy years after he was on the trail. Lucy Henderson was eighty-eight when she recounted her trail experience, claiming that her "memories of the trip are very vivid." Ruth May Fox was mentally alert enough at one hundred to dictate her recollections. She lived to be 104.

Mary Field, who spent her trail days driving oxen in 1852, lived long enough to acquire a unique distinction. Mary was interviewed in 1941:

I was 105 years old February 1, 1941. I have good health, considering my age; my appetite is fairly good. I have never worn glasses and although my eyes are failing now, as is my hearing, I am quite nimble and active in my body. I walk erect and have never used a cane. My mind is clear and my memory is good of things both past and present. . . . I am the only living witness to have actually seen and known the Prophet Joseph Smith.

Mary lived almost two more years!

—CONCLUSION—

From hopeful beginnings, through the hazards and hardships of the journey, and on to new homes and new challenges in "paradise," the young pioneers demonstrated astounding strength and courage. Many of them prospered in the fertile fields of Oregon, the sunny valleys of California, and the deserts and mountains of Utah because they were willing to work hard. Writer Horace Greeley is credited with this quote about the pioneers: "The cowards never started and the weak died on the way."

These young emigrants helped change history. They saw major changes over their lifetimes, going from the covered wagon to the steam-powered train, the automobile, and the airplane. In the 1920s Benjamin Bonney looked back on his trail days of 1845 and 1846 with nostalgia:

When I tell my grandchildren about the old days, about the plains being dark with . . . buffalo, about the Indians and the mining camps, they look at me as if I could not be telling the truth. Those old days are gone forever, and the present generation can never know the charm and romance of the old west.

Today's readers are even further removed from trail days than Benjamin's grandchildren were. But this part of the American heritage can be recaptured, in a small way, by walking along those ruts to see where young pioneers like Moses Shallenberger, Eliza Ann McAuley, George Bean, Aurelia Spencer, Welborn Beeson, and Abigail Scott made history. To discover the real story, walk along the Platte River, climb Independence Rock, pick up a buffalo chip, swat a mosquito, eat some dust, hear a wolf howl, and read the diaries. Then, perhaps, you can see the young pioneers' dramatic saga for the marvel and miracle that it was.

~

Oregon Trail ruts at Scotts Bluff National Monument, Nebraska.
—Courtesy Stanley Kimball

BIBLIOGRAPHY

This bibliography is divided into two parts. Part One lists alphabetically all the young pioneers quoted in this work and the primary and secondary sources for those quotes. Women's married names, if known, are in parentheses. Part Two is a list of other works consulted, including the sources for quotations from adult pioneers.

PART ONE

Alexander, Sara: Reminiscences. Archives, Church of Jesus Christ of Latter-day Saints Headquarters (hereafter LDS Archives), Salt Lake City.

Anderson, Agnes and Alexander: John Deviltry-Smith. "Coming to Zion: Wreck of the *Julia Ann.*" *Brigham Young University Studies* 29 (1989): 234–35.

Applegate, Jesse A.: Ruth B. Moynihan. "Children and Young People on the Overland Trail." *Western Historical Quarterly* (July 1975): 279–84. See also Lloyd W. Coffman. *Blazing a Wagon Trail to Oregon.* Enterprise, Ore.: Echo Books, 1993.

Baker, Amenzo: George W. Bean. *A Utah Pioneer of 1847 and His Family Records.* Comp. Flora Diane Bean Horne. Salt Lake City: Flora D. B. Horne, 1945.

Baker, William George: Jean Rio Baker Griffiths. "Diary of Jean Rio Baker Griffiths." LDS Archives.

Bankhead, Alex, George, Ike, John, Lewis, and Sam: Kate Carter, comp. *Our Pioneer Heritage* (hereafter *OPH*). Vol. 8. Salt Lake City: Daughters of Utah Pioneers, 1960.

Bean, George Washington: Autobiography. LDS Archives.

Beck, Margaret Simmons Bennet: *OPH.* Vol. 9.

Beeson, Welborn: Bert Webber, ed. *Welborn Beeson on the Oregon Trail in 1853.* Lake Oswego, Ore.: Smith & Smith Publishing, 1986.

Bertlesen, Nicolena Marie: *OPH.* Vol. 3. (This account was changed to first person.)

Bigler, Henry W.: *Henry Bigler Journal, 1846–99.* Berkeley: Univesity of California Press, 1962.

Black, Joseph S. and William: "Joseph S. Black Family History." LDS Archives.

Blake, F. W.: Diary. LDS Archives.

Bond, John: Leroy R. and Ann W. Hafen. *Handcarts to Zion* (hereafter *Handcarts*). Glendale, Calif.: Arthur H. Clark, 1960.

Bonney, Benjamin F.: Fred Lockley. *Conversations with Pioneer Men* (hereafter *CWPM*). Vol. 2. Comp. Mike Helm. Eugene, Ore.: Rainy Day Press, 1996.

Braly, John Hyde and Sarah: Merrill Mattes. *Platte River Road Narratives*. No. 213. Urbana: University of Illinois Press, 1988.

Brooks, Elisha: Elisha Brooks. *The Life Story of a California Pioneer*. San Francisco: Abbott-Brady Printing, 1922.

Brooks, Frank, George, and Mary: *Handcarts*.

Brown, Henry: John Brown. *The Autobiography of Pioneer John Brown*. Salt Lake City: self-published, 1941.

Bryant, Edwin: Edwin Bryant. *What I Saw in California: Being the Journal of a Tour*. New York: D. Appleton & Co., 1848.

Bunnell, Romania (Pratt Penrose): Vicky Burgess-Olsen, ed. *Sister Saints*. Provo, Utah: Brigham Young University Press, 1978.

Bunnell, Stephen I.: Stephen I. Bunnell. "Bunnell Family History." LDS Archives.

Caldwell, Agnes (Southworth): Susan Arrington Madsen. *I Walked to Zion*. Salt Lake City: Deseret Book Co., 1994.

Canfield, Lucy Marie (Margetts): Madsen. *I Walked to Zion*.

Cannon, Ann (Woodbury): Ann Cannon Woodbury. *Cannon Family Historical Treasury*. Salt Lake City: self-published, 1987.

Carpenter, Helen: Lillian Schissel. *Westward Journey: Diaries of Women on the Overland Trails* (hereafter *Westward*). New York: Schoeken Books, 1982.

Carringer, Nicholas: Dale Morgan, ed. *Overland in 1846: Diaries and Letters of the California-Oregon Trail*. Vol. 1. Georgetown, Calif.: Talisman Press, 1963.

Carson, Elvira: Autobiography. LDS Archives.

Carter, Kate B.: "The Negro Pioneer." In *OPH*. Vol. 8.

Chambers, Andrew and Mary Jane: Robert L. Munkers. "Women's Life on the Road West." *Annals of Wyoming* 42 (October 1970).

Christensen, Christian L.: Reminiscences. Harold B. Lee Library, Brigham Young University (hereafter BYU Archives), Salt Lake City.

Clark, Anna (Hale): Memoirs. LDS Archives.

Clayton, William: George D. Smith, ed. *An Intimate Chronicle: The Journals of William Clayton*. Salt Lake City: Signature Books, 1995.

Clements, Albert Nephi and Elizabeth (Kendall): *OPH*. Vol 3.

Colvig, William M.: *CWPM*. Vol. 2.

Cooke, Lucy: Kenneth L. Holmes, ed. *Covered Wagon Women* (hereafter *Covered Wagon*). Vol. 4. Glendale, Calif.: Arthur H. Clark, 1988.

Coolbrith, Ina: Todd Compton. *In Sacred Loneliness: The Plural Wives of Joseph Smith*. Salt Lake City: Signature Books, 1997. See also Daughters of Utah Pioneers, comp. *An Enduring Legacy* (hereafter *AEL*). Vol. 1. Salt Lake City: Daughters of Utah Pioneers, 1978.

Coombs, Isaiah Moses: *OPH.* Vol. 1.

Cooper, Frederick A.: *Handcarts.*

Cornwall, Joseph: Morgan, ed. *Overland in 1846.* Vol. 2.

Cox, Lucretia: Stanley Kimball. *Heber C. Kimball: Mormon Patriarch and Pioneer.* Urbana: University of Illinois Press, 1981.

Cropper, Thomas Waters: "History of Thomas Waters Cropper." LDS Archives.

Cummins, Sarah: Moynihan. "Children and Young People on the Overland Trail."

Dedrickson, Theo: *OPH.* Vol. 7.

Donner, Eliza: Morgan, ed. *Overland in 1846.* Vol 1.

Dunn, Mary Kelly: Fred Lockley. *Conversations with Pioneer Women* (hereafter *CWPW*). Vol 1. Ed. Mike Helm. Eugene, Ore.: Rainy Day Press, 1993.

Egan, Howard R.: *Pioneering the West: Major Howard Egan's Diary.* Richmond, Utah: self-published, 1917.

Ensign, Martin Luther: Ivey Hooper Hill, ed. "Autobiography of Martin Luther Ensign." In *John Ensign Hill Diaries and Biographical Material.* Logan, Utah: J. P. Smith & Son, 1962.

Fields, Mary (Garner): *OPH.* Vol. 7.

Fish, Joseph: John H. Krendel, ed. *The Life and Times of Joseph Fish, Mormon Pioneer.* Danville, Ill.: Interstate Printers & Publishers, 1970.

Flake, Liz (Rowan): *OPH.* Vol. 8. See also *AEL.* Vol. 8.

Freshwater, William Henry: *OPH.* Vol. 7.

Fry, Fanny (Simons): *AEL.* Vol. 6.

Fulkerson, Frederick Richard: Aubrey L. Haines. *Historic Sites along the Oregon Trail.* Tucson: Patrice Press, 1981.

Gardener, Amanda (Johnson): *CWPW.* Vol. 1.

Gardner, Robert R.: James Smithies. Journal. LDS Archives.

Garrison, Enoch: Edwin Bryant. *What I Saw in California: Being the Journal of a Tour.* New York: D. Appleton & Co., 1848.

Geisel, Mary (Blake): *CWPW.* Vol. 1.

Gibson, William: Journal. LDS Archives.

Godfrey, James: Peter van der Pas, ed. "The Overland Diary of James Godfrey." *Nevada County Historical Society Bulletin* 44 (1990): 17.

Goodridge, George Albert, Harriet Ann, and Sophia: *Covered Wagon.* Vol. 2.

Graehl, Eliza: Louise Graehl. *Treasures of Pioneer History.* Comp. Kate B. Carter. Vol. 4. Salt Lake City: Daughters of Utah Pioneers, 1956.

Grant, George W.: *Handcarts.*

Grover, Emmeline (Rich): Carol Madsen. *Journey to Zion: Voices from the Mormon Trail.* Salt Lake City: Deseret Book Co., 1997.

Harmon, Elmeda S.: Appleton Harmon. *Appleton Harmon Goes West*. Ed. Maybelle H. Anderson. Berkeley: Gillick Press, 1946.

Hays, Lorena L. and Sarah Louise (Whitlatch): Jeanne H. Watson, ed. *To the Land of Gold and Wickedness*. St. Louis: Patrice Press, 1990.

Hembree, Joel: Reg P. Duffin. "The Grave of Joel Hembree." *Overland Journal* 3 (Spring 1995): 6–16.

Henderson, Lettie and Lucy (Deady): *CWPW*. Vol. 1.

Hepp, Charles: Webber, ed. *Welborn Beeson*.

Hess, David C.: "Family Record and Journal of John W. Hess." LDS Archives.

Hester, Sallie (Maddock): *Covered Wagon*. Vol. 1.

Hill, Nancy Jane: Reg P. Duffin. "Here Lies Nancy Hill?" *Overland Journal* 1 (July 1983): 4–13. See also "Nancy Hill Revisited." *Overland Journal* 4 (Fall 1986): 56–64.

Huntington, C. Allen: *Handcarts*.

Hurren, Mary: Caldwell. "Autobiography of Agnes Caldwell." In Graehl. *Treasures of Pioneer History*. Vol. 5.

Jacobs, Zebulon: Diaries. LDS Archives.

James, Emma, Mary Ann, Reuben, and Sarah: Laleta Dixon. "History of My Ancestors." BYU Archives.

James, Silas and Sylvester: Jane E. Manning James. "Autoiography of Jane E. Manning James." LDS Archives.

Johnson, Mrs. Boone: *CWPW*. Vol. 1.

Jones, Albert: Lyndia McDowell Carter. "The Mormon Handcart Companies." *Overland Journal* 13 (Spring 1995): 5–12.

Jones, Mary Ann (Ellsworth): Madsen. *Journey to Zion*.

Judd, Margaret Gay (Clawson): Reminiscences. LDS Archives.

Judd, Mary Minerva D.: *OPH*. Vol. 7. See also Mattes. *Platte River Road Narratives*. No. 855.

Judson, Phoebe Goodell: John M. McClelland Jr., ed. *A Pioneer's Search for an Ideal Home*. Bellingham, Wash.: self-published, 1925.

Kantner, Mrs. W. C.: *CWPW*. Vol 1.

Keegan, Elizabeth (Ketchum): *Covered Wagon*. Vol. 4.

Keil, William: Mattes. *Platte River Road Narratives*. No. 1526. See also Ruth Anderson. "Music on the Move: Instruments on the Western Frontier." *Overland Journal* 3 (Spring 1987): 27–34.

Kimball, David P.: *Handcarts*.

King, Hannah Tapfield: *Covered Wagon*. Vol. 6.

Knight, Lucy, Plutarch, and Seneca: *Westward*. See also "Diary of an Oregon Pioneer of 1853." *Transactions of the Oregon Pioneer* (1928): 38–56.

Lambkin, William: Georgia Willis Read and Ruth Gaines, eds. *Gold Rush: The Journals, Drawings and Other Papers of J. Goldsborough Bruff.* Vol. 2. New York: Columbia University Press, 1944.

Leavitt, Dudley and Thomas: Juanita Leavitt Brooks, ed. *History of Sarah Studevant Leavitt.* Salt Lake City: n.p., 1965.

Lenox, Edward Henry and Frances: Edward Henry Lenox. "Recollections." In *Overland to Oregon.* Ed. Robert Whitaker. Oakland: n.p., 1904.

Lithgow, Louisa: Watson, ed. *To the Land of Gold and Wickedness.*

Loader, Patience and Sarah: John Jaques. *Life History and Writings of John Jaques.* Ed. Stella Jaques Bell. Rexburg, Idaho: Ricks College Press, 1978.

Loba, Jean Frederick: Journal, 1899. Knox College Archives, Galesburg, Ill.

Logan-Flood, Cloye Burnett: *Westward.*

Masters, Andrew Jackson: *CWPM.* Vol 2.

May, Ruth (Fox): *OPH.* Vol. 7.

McAuley, Eliza Ann (Egbert): *Covered Wagon.* Vol. 4.

McBride, Heber: Autobiography. BYU Archives.

McBride, Jeanette, Maggie, and Peter: *OPH.* Vol. 13.

McDaniel, Kate (Furniss): Watson, ed. *To the Land of Gold and Wickedness.*

McIntyre, Thomas: "Journal: Handcart Reminiscences." LDS Archives.

McKean, Eliza (Hustler): *CWPW.* Vol. 1.

McNeil, Margaret (Ballard): *OPH.* Vol. 3.

McWilliams, John: John McWilliams. *Recollections of His Youth Experience in California and Civil War.* Princeton, N.J.: n.p., n.d.

Mechan, Lucina (Boren): Graehl. *Treasures of Pioneer History.* Vol. 6.

Miller, Jacob: Bean. *A Utah Pioneer of 1847 and His Family Records.* See also Jacob Miller. "Journal of Jacob Miller." LDS Archives.

Mineer, Alma Elizabeth (Felt): *AEL.* Vol. 7.

Morrison, Martha Ann: *Westward.*

Moulding, Sarah Sophia (Gledhill): Autobiography. Utah State University Archives, Logan, Utah.

Mount, Mary Jane (Tanner): Autobiography. LDS Archives.

Normington, Mary Ellen: Evelyn May Cook Cox. "They Left a Heritage of Faith and Courage." LDS Archives. (This account has been changed to first person.)

Norris, Sarah Louisa: Carol Madsen. *In Their Own Words: Women and the Story of Nauvoo.* Salt Lake City: Deseret Book Co., 1994.

Nutting, Rebecca (Woodson): *Westward.*

Ohmart, Valeda W. Smith: *CWPW.* Vol. 1.

Oldroyd, Mary Anderson: Kate B. Carter, comp. *Heart Throbs of the West.* Vol. 9. Salt Lake City: Daughters of Utah Pioneers, 1948.

Ormond, William M. and Lorenzo D.: Read and Gaines, eds. *Gold Rush.* Vol. 2.

Parker, Arthur: *Handcarts.*

Perkins, Ben, Mary Ann, and Sarah: *OPH.* Vol. 8.

Perkins, Emma (Hembree): *CWPW.* Vol. 1.

Pettit, Edwin: Edwin Pettit. *Biography of Edwin Pettit, 1834–1912.* Salt Lake City: Arrow Press, 1912.

Powell, Mary (Sabin): Madsen. *Journey to Zion.*

Pringle, Octavius: Morgan, ed. *Overland in 1846.*

Pucell, Margaret and Ellen: Recollections. LDS Archives. See also Daniel W. Jones. *Forty Years among the Indians.* Salt Lake City: Juvenile Instructor Office, 1890.

Quick, Rhoda (Johnson): *CWPW.* Vol. 1.

Reed, Patty: *Covered Wagon.* Vol. 1. See also Bernard DeVoto. *The Year of Decision, 1846.* Boston: Little Brown & Co., 1942.

Reed, Virginia (Murphy): *Covered Wagon.* Vol. 1. See also Daniel D. Holt. "Had I Remained with the Company . . ." *Overland Journal* 14 (Winter 1996–97): 17–27.

Rhoads, Catherine (Sheldon) and Sarah (Daylor): *AEL.* Vol. 1.

Roberts, B. H.: Gary Bergara, ed. *The Autobiography of B. H. Roberts.* Salt Lake City: Signature Press, 1990.

Roberts, Robert D.: Reminiscence. LDS Archives. See also Carter. "The Mormon Handcart Companies."

Rogers, Barsina: Diary, 1867. Huntington Library, San Marino, Calif.

Rogerson, Josiah: *Handcarts.*

Rowan, Alice and Byron: *AEL.* Vol. 8.

Sager, Catherine (Pringle), Elizabeth (Helm), Francis, John, and Matilda (Delaney): Catherine, Elizabeth and Matilda Sager. *The Whitman Massacre of 1847.* Fairfield, Wash.: Ye Galleon Press, 1981. See also *CWPW.* Vol. 1.

Schallenberger, Moses: Charles K. Graydon. "Trail of the First Wagons over the High Sierra." *Overland Journal* 4 (Winter 1986): 4–17. See also George R. Stewart. *The California Trail.* Lincoln: University of Nebraska Press, 1962. See also Moses Schallenberger. *The Opening of the California Trail: The Story of the Stevens Party from the Reminiscences of Moses Schallenberger.* Berkeley: University of California Press, 1953.

Scott, Abigail (Duniway), Etty, Harvey, Kate, and Margaret: *Covered Wagon.* Vol. 5.

Shepherd, Elizabeth (Holtgrieve): *CWPW.* Vol. 2.

Simpson, Barnet: *CWPM.* Vol. 2.

Smith, Jesse Nathaniel: Oliver R. Smith, ed. *Six Decades in the Early West: The Journal of Jesse Nathaniel Smith.* Provo, Utah: Oliver R. Smith, 1970.

Smith, John: Autobiography. LDS Archives.

Smith, Josephine: See Ina Coolbrith.

Smith, Lot: Stanley B. Kimball. *The Mormon Battalion on the Santa Fe Trail, 1846.* Santa Fe: National Park Service, 1996.

Smith, Louisa: *Westward.*

Smithies, James: Journals. LDS Archives.

Spencer, Aurelia (Rogers): *Life Sketches.* Salt Lake City: Geo. Q. Cannon & Sons, 1898.

Steele, John: John Steele. *Across the Plains in 1850.* Ed. John Schafer. Chicago: Caxton Club, 1930.

Stewart, Harriet Augusta: *Covered Wagon.* Vol. 7.

Stewart, Helen (Love): *Diary of Helen M. Stewart, 1853.* Springfield, Ore.: Lane County Historical Society, 1961.

Stoddard, James: Archer Walters. Journal. LDS Archives. See also *Handcarts.*

Stoughton, John: Coffman. *Blazing a Wagon Trail to Oregon.*

Stuart, Granville: Granville Stuart. *Forty Years on the Frontier.* Ed. Paul C. Phillips. Glendale, Calif.: Arthur H. Clark, 1957.

Sweeten, Robert: "Robert Sweeten Family Reunion Newsletter, 1961." LDS Archives.

Tetherow, Sam: *CWPM.* Vol. 2.

Thomas, Catherine (Morris): *CWPW.* Vol. 1.

Todd, Caroline: Haines. *Historic Sites along the Oregon Trail.*

True, Charles Frederick and Carro: Sally Ralston True, ed. *The Overland Memoir of Charles Frederick True.* Independence, Mo.: Oregon-California Trails Association, 1993.

Veatch, Robert M.: *CWPW.* Vol. 2.

Ward, Ann (King): *OPH.* Vol. 5. (This account has been changed to first person.)

Ward, Frankie: Watson, ed. *To the Land of Gold and Wickedness.*

Warner, Mary E.: Diary. Bancroft Library, Berkeley, Calif. (This diary is often confused with that of her sister-in-law, also named Mary.)

Washburn, Marilla R. (Bailey): *CWPW.* Vol. 1.

Weatherby, Jacob: Smith. *Six Decades in the Early West.*

White, Bernard: William Hartley. "Bernard's Boots." *New Era* (July 1983): 9–12.

Williams, Henry and Louisa: Steele. *Across the Plains in 1850.*

Williamson, Mary: Carter. "The Mormon Handcart Companies."

Woodruff, Susan: Wilford Woodruff. *Wilford Woodruff's Journals, 1833–1898.* Ed. Scott G. Kenney. Vol. 3. Salt Lake City: Signature Books, 1983.

Woolley, Rachel Emma (Simmons): Carter, comp. *Heart Throbs*. Vol. 11.

Zieber, Eugenia: *Covered Wagon*. Vol. 3.

PART TWO

Books

Arrington, Leonard. *Charles C. Rich*. Provo, Utah: Brigham Young University Press, 1974.

————, and Susan Arrington Madsen. *Sunbonnet Sisters: True Stories of Mormon Women and Frontier Life*. Salt Lake City: Bookcraft, 1984.

Beecher, Maureen Ursenbach, ed. *The Personal Writings of Eliza Roxcy Snow*. Salt Lake City: University of Utah Press, 1995.

Bitten, Davis. *Guide to Mormon Diaries and Autobiographies*. Provo, Utah: Brigham Young University Press, 1977.

Brooks, Juanita. *On the Mormon Frontier: The Diary of Hosea Stout*. Vol. 1, 1844–1861. Salt Lake City: University of Utah Press, 1964.

Bullock, Thomas. *Kingdom in the West: The Mormons and the American Frontier*. Ed. Will Bagley. Spokane, Wash.: Arthur H. Clark Co., 1997.

Clark, Thomas D., ed. *Gold Rush Diary: Being the Journal of Elisha Douglass Perkins on the Overland Trail in the Spring and Summer of 1849*. Lexington: University of Kentucky, 1967.

Clyman, James. Ed. Charles L. Camp. *James Clyman, Frontiersman*. Portland, Ore.: n.p., 1960.

Cross, Mary Bywater. *Treasures in the Trunk: Quilts of the Oregon Trail*. Nashville: Rutledge Hill Press, 1993.

Drury, Clifford. *First White Women Over the Rockies*. Vol. 2. Glendale, Calif.: Arthur H. Clark, 1963.

Durham, Alfred M., comp. *Pioneer Songs*. Salt Lake City: Daughters of Utah Pioneers, 1932.

Faragher, John Mack. *Women and Men on the Overland Trail*. New Haven: Yale University Press, 1979.

Fish, Joseph. *The Pioneers of the Southwest and Rocky Mountain Regions*. Salt Lake City: Seymour P. Fish, 1972.

Franzwa, Gregory. *The Oregon Trail Revisited*. Gerald, Mo.: Patrice Press, 1983.

————. *Maps of the Oregon Trail*. Gerald, Mo.: Patrice Press, 1982.

————. *Maps of the California Trail*. Tucson: Patrice Press, 1999.

Godfrey, Kenneth and Audrey M., and Jill Mulvay Derr. *Women's Voices: An Untold History of the Latter-day Saints*. Salt Lake City: Deseret Book Co., 1982.

Grant, Bruce. *Concise Encyclopedia of the American Indian*. New York: Bonanza Books, 1989.

Hill, William E. *The California Trail Yesterday and Today*. Boulder: Pruett Publishing Co., 1986.

Kane, Thomas L. *The Mormons: Nauvoo in 1848*. 1850. Reprint, Provo, Utah: David C. Martin, 1975.

Kimball, Stanley B. *Historic Resource Study: Mormon Pioneer National Historic Trail*. Washington D.C.: National Park Service, 1991.

———. *Historic Sites and Markers along the Mormon and Other Great Western Trails*. Urbana: University of Illinois Press, 1988.

———, and Violet T. Kimball. *Mormon Trail, Voyage of Discovery: The Story Behind the Scenery*. Las Vegas: KC Publications, 1995.

Mattes, Merrill J. *The Great Platte River Road*. Lincoln: Nebraska State Historical Society, 1969.

McGoffin, Susan Shelby. *Down the Santa Fe Trail and into Mexico*. Ed. Stella M. Drumm. Lincoln: University of Nebraska Press, 1962.

Monaghan, Jay. *The Overland Trail*. New York: Bobbs-Merrill Co., 1947.

Morgan, Dale L., ed. *The Overland Diary of James A. Pritchard*. Denver: Old West Publishing Co., 1959.

Morrison, Kenneth M. "The American Revolution: The Indian Story." In *Myth America: A Historical Anthology*. St. James, N.Y.: Brandywine Press, 1997.

Murphy, Dan. *Oregon Trail: Voyage of Discovery*. Las Vegas: KC Publications, 1991.

Myres, Sandra L. *Westering Women and the Frontier Experience 1800–1915*. Albuquerque: University of New Mexico Press, 1982.

National Park Service. *Comprehensive Management and Use Plan, California National Historic Trail, Pony Express National Historic Trail, Oregon National Historic Trail and Mormon Pioneer National Historic Trail*. Washington D.C.: National Park Service, 1999.

Newell, Linda King, and Valeen Tippetts Avery. *Mormon Enigma: Emma Hale Smith*. Garden City, N.J.: Doubleday & Co., 1984.

Parkman, Francis. *The Oregon Trail*. New York: New American Library, 1978.

Parrish, Randall. *The Great Plains*. Chicago: A. C. McClurg & Co., 1915.

Peters, Arthur King. *Seven Trails West*. New York: Abbeville Press, 1996.

Piercy, Frederick. *Route from Liverpool to Great Salt Lake Valley*. Ed. Fawn M. Brodie. Cambridge, Mass.: Harvard University Press, 1962.

Read, George Willis. *A Pioneer of 1850: 1819–1880*. Ed. Georgia Willis Read. Boston: Little, Brown & Co., 1927.

Ross, Nancy Wilson. *Westward the Women*. New York: Random House, 1958.

Russell, Marian. *Memoirs of Marian Russell along the Santa Fe Trail*. Evanston, Ill.: Branding Iron Press, 1954.

Smith, George D., ed. *An Intimate Chronicle: The Journals of William Clayton.* Salt Lake City: Signature Books, 1995.

Smucker, Samuel M., ed. *The Life of Col. John Charles Fremont, and His Narrative of Explorations and Adventures.* New York and Auburn, N.Y.: Miller, Orton & Mulligan, 1856.

Stegner, Wallace. *The Gathering of Zion.* New York: McGraw Hill, 1971.

Stratton, Joanna L. *Pioneer Women: Voices from the Kansas Frontier.* New York: Simon and Schuster, 1981.

Tullidge, Edward W. *The Women of Mormondom.* Salt Lake City: self-published, 1877.

Unruh, John D. *The Plains Across.* Urbana: University of Illinois Press, 1979.

Van Wagoner, Richard S. *Mormon Polygamy: A History.* Salt Lake City: Signature Books, 1992.

Whitman, Narcissa. *The Letters of Narcissa Whitman, 1836–1847.* Fairfield, Wash.: Ye Galleon Press, 1986.

Winn, Kenneth H. *Exiles in a Land of Liberty: Mormons in America 1830–1846.* Chapel Hill: University of North Carolina Press, 1989.

Worcester, Don, ed. *Pioneer Trails West.* Caldwell, Idaho: Caxton Printers, 1985.

Periodicals

Applegate, Lindsay. "The Applegate Trail: Notes and Reminiscences of Laying Out and Establishing the Old Emigrant Road into Southern Oregon, 1846." *Overland Journal* 11 (Spring 1993): 2–23.

Beckham, Stephen D. "The Barlow Road." *Overland Journal* 2 (Fall 1984): 5–42.

Brown, Sharon. "What the Covered Wagon Covered." *Overland Journal* 4 (Fall 1986): 32–39.

Christy, Howard A. "Weather, Disaster, and Responsibility: An Essay on the Willie and Martin Handcart Story." *BYU Studies* 37 (1, 1997–98): 6–74.

Gibbons, Boyd. "Oregon Trail: The Itch to Move West." *National Geographic.* Vol. 170, No. 2 (August 1986).

Hunt, Thomas H. "A Massacre: Bloody Point, 1852." *Overland Journal* 7 (Fall 1989): 2–25.

Kimball, Stanley B. "Sail and Rail Pioneers." *BYU Studies* 35 (2, 1995): 6–42.

Kimball, Violet T. "Daughters of Zion: Mormon Women on the Trek West." *Cobblestone* (May 1997): 26-29.

———."Mary Richardson Walker: Sidesaddle and Pregnant to Oregon in 1838." *Overland Journal* 13 (Winter 1995–96): 4–10.

———. "Work and Play: The Trail through the Eyes of Young Pioneers." *Cobblestone* (May 1997): 20-23.

Martin, Charles, and Charles W. Martin Jr. "The Fourth of July: A Holiday on the Trail." *Overland Journal* 10 (Summer 1992): 2–20.

Martin, Charles W., Jr. "The Lighter Side of the Trail Experience." *Overland Journal* 5 (Fall 1987): 7–13.

Mattes, Merrill J. "A Look Back at the Beginnings of OCTA and Its Contributions over the Years." *Overland Journal* 13 (Winter 1995–96): 21–28.

Munkres, Robert L. "Devil's Gate." *Overland Journal* 7 (Spring 1989): 2–18.

Myers, Sandra L. "I Too Have Seen the Elephant: Women on the Overland Trails." *Overland Journal* 4 (Winter 1986): 25–33.

Rau, Weldon Willis. "Across Today's Oregon State, 1852." *Overland Journal* 16 (Spring 1998): 4–19.

Rieck, Richard L. "A Geography of Death on the Oregon-California Trail, 1840–1860." *Overland Journal* 9 (Spring 1991): 13–21.

———. "Geography of the Oregon Trail West of Fort Hall." *Overland Journal* 17 (Summer 1999): 9–22.

Walker, Margaret F. "A Woman's Work Is Never Done: Or, the Dirt on Men and Their Laundry." *Overland Journal* 16 (Summer 1998): 4–13.

Watson, Jeanne H. "Women's Travails and Triumphs on the Overland Trails." *Overland Journal* 9 (Winter 1991): 28–36.

———. "The Carson Emigrant Road." *Overland Journal* 4 (Fall 1980): 4–12.

Williams, Carol. "My First Indian: Interaction between Women and Indians on the Trail, 1845–1865." *Overland Journal* 4 (Fall 1986): 13–18.

Young, Brigham. *Millennial Star* 18 (January 26, 1856): 122–24.

Newspapers
Alton (Illinois) *Telegraph*, 1846.
Aurora (Ohio) *Guardian*, 1854.
Kanesville (Iowa) *Frontier Guardian*, 1849–1852.
Nauvoo (Illinois) *Expositor*, April 1844.
Nauvoo (Illinois) *Times and Seasons*, 1844–46.
St. Louis Daily Evening Gazette, 1844.
St. Louis Republican, 1847–48.
St. Louis Weekly Reveille, 1846–47.
Warsaw (Illinois) *Signal*, 1845.

Other
"California," poem by Ina Coolbrith. In *AEL*, vol. 1.
"Handcart Song," words by J. D. T. McAllister. In Durham, comp., *Pioneer Songs*.

"I Have Something Sweet to Tell You," poem by Frances S. Osgood, c. 1852. Music by C. C. Converse. Courtesy Special Collections, Dartmouth College Library. Hanover, N.H.

"A Pioneer Campfire Song," words and music by Evan Stephans. In Durham, comp., *Pioneer Songs.*

"Whoa, Haw, Buck and Jerry Boy," song passed down by oral tradition to Stanley Kimball.

Index

217

wolves, 79, 137, 168, 169

women's rights. *See* feminism; suffrage movement, women's

Woodruff, Susan, 132

Woodruff, Wilford, 38, 132, 168

Woolley, Rachel Emma, 72, 75, 83, 165, 169, 195, 202

Young, Brigham, 4, 10, 29, 43, 196

Zachary, Mary, 117

Zion, 4. *See also* Mormons; Salt Lake Valley

Violet T. Kimball is a self-described "trail nut" who has traveled and photographed all the major overland trails. A former opera singer, she has been a freelance writer and photographer since 1970 and has won awards for her work. She has written for dozens of local and national publications on topics as diverse as history, quilting, beauty, farming, stamps, and travel. Her first book, *The Mormon Trail: The Story Behind the Scenery*, was published in 1995. She resides in St. George, Utah, with her husband Stanley.

Teacher's Guide for

STORIES OF
Young Pioneers

In Their Own Words

The Teacher's Guide for Stories of Young Pioneers is free with the purchase of a book. If you would like to receive the Teacher's Guide only, please use the order for on the following page and send $3.00 for shipping and handling.

We encourage you to patronize your local bookstore. Most stores will order any title they do not stock. You may also order directly from Mountain Press, using the order form provided below or by calling our toll-free, 24-hour number.

Young Adult and Children's titles of interest:

YOUNG ADULT

_____ Bold Women in Michigan's History	paper/$12.00
_____Crazy Horse: A Photographic Biography	paper/$20.00
_____Custer: A Photographic Biography	paper/$24.00
_____Lewis and Clark: A Photographic Journey	paper/$18.00
_____The Oregon Trail: A Photographic Journey	paper/$18.00
_____The Pony Express: A Photographic History	paper/$22.00
_____Sacagawea's Son: The Life of Jean Baptiste Charbonneau	paper/$10.00
_____Smoky: The Cowhorse	paper/$16.00
_____Stories of Young Pioneers: In Their Own Words	paper/$14.00
_____What's So Great About Granite?	paper/$18.00

CHILDREN

_____Awesome Osprey: Fishing Birds of the World	paper/$12.00
_____Blind Tom: The Horse Who Helped Build the Great Railroad	paper/$10.00
_____The Charcoal Forest: How Fire Helps Animals and Plants	paper/$12.00
_____Cowboy in the Making	cloth/$15.00
_____Glacier National Park: An ABC Adventure	paper/$10.00
_____Loons: Diving Birds of the North	paper/$12.00
_____My First Horse	paper/$16.00
_____Nature's Yucky! Gross Stuff That Helps Nature Work	paper/$10.00
_____Nature's Yucky 2! The Desert Southwest	paper/$12.00
_____Owls: Whoo Are They?	paper/$12.00
_____Snowy Owls: Whoo Are They?	cloth/$12.00
_____Spotted Bear: A Rocky Mountain Folktale	cloth/$15.00
_____Three Dogs, Two Mules, and a Reindeer	cloth/$15.00
_____The Will James Cowboy Book	cloth/$18.00
_____You Can Be a Nature Detective	paper/$14.00
_____Young Cowboy	cloth/$15.00

Please include $3.50 for 1-4 books, $5.00 for 5 or more books to cover shipping and handling.

Send the books marked above. I enclose $_____

Name _____

Address _____

City/State/Zip _____

☐ Payment enclosed (check or money order in U.S. funds)

Bill my: ☐VISA ☐MasterCard ☐Discover ☐American Express

Card No._____

Security Code #_____   Expiration Date _____

Signature _____

MOUNTAIN PRESS PUBLISHING COMPANY
P. O. Box 2399 • Missoula, MT 59806 • Fax 406-728-1635
Order Toll Free **1-800-234-5308** • *Have your credit card ready*
E-mail: info@mtnpress.com • Web site: www.mountain-press.com

Breinigsville, PA USA
17 June 2010
240086BV00001B/3/P